Contents

v

46   ARTICLE V: DUTIES OF OFFICERS

54   ARTICLE VI: MEETINGS

60   ARTICLE VII: BOARD OF DIRECTORS

Bylaws Workbook
A Handbook for New & Established Societies
Second Edition

Compiled by Marcia S. Lindley
Revised by Roberta "Bobbi" King

Federation of Genealogical Societies

Bylaws Workbook: A Handbook for New & Established Societies

Editor: Roberta "Bobbi" King
Production Editor: Lisa A. Alzo, MFA
Cover and interior design: Susan Zacharias

Federation of Genealogical Societies
P.O. Box 200940
Austin, TX 78720-0940

Printed in the United States of America
First Printing 1996
Second printing 2012

About the Authors

The first edition of this bylaws workbook was compiled and edited by Marcia S. Lindley, an active member of the Arizona State Genealogical Society, serving a variety of positions including president, vice president, director and member of the editorial board. Lindley was responsible for leading a group of society members in an extensive review of their bylaws. She is a staff attorney with the Court of Appeals of the State of Arizona and holds degrees in history and law.

The second edition was compiled and edited by Roberta "Bobbi" King, for several years a member of the FGS board of directors, as well as serving as vice president of administration and parliamentarian. She is a member of the bylaws committee and the bylaws review committee, for which she has reviewed dozens of society bylaws. On the publications committee, she is editor of the *Society Strategies Series* papers. She is associated with several Colorado genealogical societies, as well as a member of the National Genealogical Society and the Association of Professional Genealogists (APG). King was recipient of the *APGQ* Award of Excellence in 2008.

Acknowledgments

A number of member societies of the Federation of Genealogical Societies were asked to submit their bylaws for use as examples. Those that participated were:

Arizona Genealogical Advisory Board
Arizona State Genealogical Society Inc.
Blair Society for Genealogical Research
Bunker Family Association of America
California Genealogical Society
Colorado Council of Genealogical Societies
Colorado Genealogical Society
Computer-Assisted Genealogy Group of Northern Illinois
Dearborn Genealogical Society
Durham-Orange Genealogical Society
East Cuyahoga County Genealogical Society
Eastern Washington Genealogical Society
Eaton County Genealogical Society
Elkhart County Genealogical Society
Fairfax Genealogical Society
Genealogical Society of Riverside
Genealogical Workshop of Mesa Inc.
Gentech Inc.
Green Valley Genealogical Society
Hamilton County Chapter of the Ohio Genealogical Society
International Society for British Genealogy and Family History
Iowa Genealogical Society
Lake County Genealogical Society
Larimer County Genealogical Society Inc.
Lee County Genealogy Society Inc.
Minnesota Genealogical Society Inc.
Polish Genealogical Society of America
San Antonio Genealogical and Historical Society
South Bay Cities Genealogical Society
St. Clair County Genealogical Society
Treasure Coast Genealogical Society Inc.

The Federation would like to thank Phyllis Brown Miller of the Ohio Genealogical Society for critiquing the first edition of this book and Gary Mokotoff of the Jewish Genealogical Society Inc. who produced the first edition.

The second edition was edited and produced by Roberta "Bobbi" King, with assistance from Jana Broglin, cg, and Matthew Wright. Additional edits by Lisa A. Alzo, mfa.

vii

102   HIERARCHY OF SOCIETY DOCUMENTS

105   WHEN DISCIPLINARY ACTION IS CALLED FOR

112   ELECTRONIC MEETINGS

117   VOTING AND ELECTRONIC VOTING

Preface

The following was prepared by Frederick E. Moss, JD, LLM

Fred serves, capably and generously, as the legal advisor to the board of directors of FGS. When the board convenes its first meeting with the newly elected board members, Fred offers an orientation reminding new and incumbent board members of the responsibilities and obligations inherent to board positions.

His advice also applies to the boards of directors serving the ordinary societies. From very small groups meeting at local adult education centers, to large organizations encompassing national membership, his words just as aptly apply today as they did a few years ago.

What your board needs to know
Introduction
Corporate officers have been much in the news in recent years. Scandals involving officer malfeasance and inadequate director oversight have prompted significant legislative changes in the governance of publicly held corporations. Although most legislation has not yet specifically addressed the nonprofit corporate community, a new emphasis is focused upon the role of boards of directors in general that provides a new frame of reference for considering their duties.

Director orientation
To the extent that being a director on the board of a genealogical organization set up as a not-for-profit corporation was ever viewed as a mere honorary position, clearly these positions are destined to take on a much more active role. A key first step toward preparing to effectively serve in this position is to become aware of the expanding role directors are likely to be expected to perform. Orientation should include a review of the mission, purposes and functions of the organization, and training in the basic duties of a director, namely, the duty of care and the duty of loyalty.

Duty of care
A director is expected to be reasonably informed and to actively participate in decisions made by the governing board of the organization. Normally, this is done by regular attendance at periodic meetings of the board of directors and involvement in its deliberations. All actions taken are expected to be based upon a good faith belief that the proposed course of action is in the corporation's best interest. A director is expected to conform to that standard of care that would be exercised by an "ordinary prudent person," a word of art.

Duty of loyalty
Several aspects of the duty a director owes to the organization include dealing with potential conflicts of interest and the concept of corporate opportunity. It is important to

realize that the existence of an apparent conflict of interest should not come as a surprise if any of your board members are professionally involved in any of the areas for which the organization was created to encourage. The same background that may make an individual valuable as a member of the board may also place him or her in a position where the owner's commercial enterprise may be interested in pursuing for profit an activity that the nonprofit organization might view as a corporate fund raising opportunity. The existence of an apparent conflict between the director's personal interests, and his duty to act in the corporation's best interest, does not suggest unethical behavior but does raise potential issues, which may need to be addressed (in a variety of ways).

Normally, only the President/CEO or a designated spokesperson is authorized to "speak" for an incorporated organization. Directors should normally treat the discussions occurring at board meetings with the strictest confidentiality, and avoid situations in which their individual remarks might be misunderstood as reflecting an official position of the organization.

Taxation issues

Most genealogical societies are organized under the provisions of state laws intended to qualify them for special tax treatment under the federal tax laws. In addition to exemption from the federal income tax attributable to the corporation, donations made to organizations created and operated to promote certain purposes may allow donors to deduct from their taxable income their qualifying contributions. Some of the issues that may arise from this special status and certain limitations on permissible activities that may flow from it should be made clear to board members.

Best practices for effective meetings

The board's fundamental understanding of parliamentary procedures and the principles of effective meeting management will assure expedited business transactions as well as satisfied and confident board members. Tips regarding agendas, minutes, project management, effective committees, conducting meetings, and the like may be found in numerously available references.

Other resources

- FGS *Society Strategies Series*, visit http://www.fgs.org for these and other FGS publications.

- Conference syllabi from past FGS conferences frequently address society management issues. Audiotapes may also be available.

- American Bar Association, *Guidebook for Directors of Nonprofit Corporations* (2nd Edition).

- FGS Radio, called "My Society" at http://www.fgs.org is a broadcast that focuses on the many issues confronting genealogical societies today.

Introduction

Whether they know it or not, the most important document for the members of a genealogical society is the bylaws. If the society is incorporated, the article of incorporation (also known as articles of association or charter, depending on your state's terminology) is an important document between the society and the state. The letter from the Internal Revenue Service giving the society tax-exempt status is important, as well, but the only document that tells the members how the society is supposed to function day-to-day is the bylaws. It is a task requiring careful thought and attention to detail. For that reason, you will need to spend considerable time and effort in drafting the bylaws.

Time spent crafting the details in the bylaws can save confusion, dissension, and disagreement over the long run. If you draft the bylaws with precise language, having carefully thought out exactly how your officers, board of directors, and committees should function, chances are you will resolve many questions that arise with a simple response, "What do the bylaws say?" If members can turn to the bylaws and find an easy-to-read, satisfactory answer, your society should run smoothly and well, and no one should feel left out of the process.

This workbook is intended not only for new societies that want to follow correct procedure, but also for established societies that are not certain whether their bylaws are complete, up-to-date, or clear enough. Any active society, simply because it is active, will need to revise its bylaws periodically by appointing a committee to examine each provision to see whether it still serves the purpose for which it was originally drafted and whether it reflects the way the society really operates.

Note: Planning ahead saves time and trouble. Revisions take time and are sometimes controversial.

1

Note: To incorporate or not to incorporate? See page 91 for more information on this topic.

Even between periodic revisions, which ought to occur every few years, your society will probably need to amend a provision or two for any number of reasons. You may have tried an experimental activity when you revised your bylaws but have since learned it did not work and may need to amend the bylaws to delete the provision. Or you may need to change a committee's duties, finding that things will work better if you add some duties or shift some to another committee. Or you might have found a good idea from another society that you want to try for your society.

In any event, you should consider bylaws a process rather than a finished work of art. As societies grow and change, they take on new activities and respond to new technology. In turn, officers must respond by adjusting the governing document to address the growth and changes, and the working on the bylaws will be a continual process. On the other hand, bylaws should be reasonably difficult to amend so societies are not tempted to change them every meeting. Just as the original document should be carefully thought out and drafted, so too should any amendments. If the bylaws provisions are flexible enough, they can accommodate certain changes without requiring amendments. If they are changed too often, no one will know how the society is supposed to operate and chaos may result. Societies, therefore, need to work at maintaining order while still adapting to change.

Workbook organization

This workbook was prepared based on comments and suggestions from *Robert's Rules of Order Newly Revised* and by taking examples from the bylaws of a number of FGS member societies that were gracious enough to submit copies for use in this project. Their cooperation has been invaluable. Sometimes, an example has been used that has been edited to conform to suggested drafting techniques and to make the provision more readable.

The essence of the society's provision, however, has been retained. Sometimes, an example is used with a comment noting a deficiency in the sample. Generally, that means that the example was a good one in nearly all respects, but future drafters have been alerted to a missing phrase or section that should also be included according to RONR.

The workbook is organized by sections covering each major bylaws provision in the order in which RONR recommends it appear in the bylaws. Some articles may not apply if your society is incorporated, however. You will have to decide which articles your society needs, and the numbering in your bylaws will follow those decisions.

Even if you are planning to revise only one article in your bylaws, it is recommended that you at least glance through the comments in the rest of the chapters as some comments apply to more than one article, but appear in only one chapter.

▶ **Tip:** *Robert's Rules of Order Newly Revised* is the most widely used parliamentary manual among societies. "RONR" is a common abbreviation for this reference, as will be used throughout this book.

A word of caution: The examples are included to offer ideas for provisions and to suggest appropriate language for various types of provisions. They should not just be lifted verbatim and placed in your bylaws. With the single exception of the article on adopting *Robert's Rules of Order Newly Revised* as your parliamentary authority, you will need to adapt the examples to your particular society and its unique circumstances.

The syntax of some of the examples was changed from that which existed in the actual bylaws for the purpose of creating uniformity in this book.

Watch for comments that apply expressly to incorporated societies. They will include the phrase: "if your society is incorporated."

4

Language

You will notice that the text of this workbook contains contractions and informal language. The bylaws examples, however, contain neither. Formal language should be used in bylaws. That means no contractions, no slang, and no catch phrases. It does not mean, however, that the language must be stilted, difficult to understand, or full of legalese. Provisions can, and should, be worded in simple, but precise, English, and they should be written so members can easily understand them.

A comment about grammar: It is important that the language used in bylaws be as precise as possible. Do not be afraid to use a dictionary while drafting. Running a spell check program is essential, but do not rely on it to do anything more than to correct the spelling of words. It cannot tell you whether the word you have chosen is the wrong one. Look for common mistakes, such as:

- "its" is the possessive, "it's" is the contraction; because bylaws should not contain contractions, "it's" should not appear in them;

- "statute" is a law enacted by a legislature; "statue" is an artist's representation of someone or something;

- "therefore" means "for that reason"; "therefor" means "for that"; therefore, proper usage means that your bylaws may require a five-day notice of a special meeting stating the reason therefor;

- despite the way it appears in the current version of RONR, "ex officio" is not hyphenated; "ex" with a hyphen means "former"; "ex officio" means "by virtue of the office";

- a "signatory" is a person who is authorized to sign something;

- do not spell out numbers followed by the Arabic numeral in parentheses; it clutters up your bylaws and labels them old-fashioned; just spell out numbers to ninety-nine; 100 and above should appear as Arabic numerals;

5

Note: An apostrophe can make a big difference in the meaning of a word.

■ **Old:** "...ten (10) members..."

■ **New:** "...ten members..."

- if you say "five days' notice" of something is required, note that days is possessive (to substitute for the missing "of");
- "nonprofit," "subcommittee," and the like are now written without a hyphen;
- avoid using "such," "said," and "same"; they sound like legalese and put readers off; use a pronoun or an article instead; "the" or "those" can be just fine;
- the appropriate pronoun for a board of directors, a committee, or a society is "it," not "they."

Note: Attorneys are valuable consultants., but often write in legalese. Choose your best editor to oversee creation of your bylaws document.

Throughout this workbook, a comma is used to separate items in a series, including the last item. Although modern usage generally omits the final comma, that practice can occasionally lead to confusion and misinterpretation. Because bylaws need to be precise, it is recommended that you include the final comma to promote the utmost in clarity.

Drafting suggestions

Use consistent terms throughout your bylaws. If you call your governing board the Executive Board, continue to use that term; do not call it the Executive Board on one page and the Executive Council on another. If you list the "purposes" of your society, do not call them "objects" in a later section. If you call it a general membership meeting in the article on meetings, do not call it a regular society business meeting elsewhere.

Use parallel construction when possible. If you list four duties of a committee, make sure the initial verb for each duty is the same type of verb. Do not use, for instance: "The committee shall be responsible for distribution of documents and for sending notices." Make it instead:

"The committee shall be responsible for distributing . . . and for sending . . . ." If you introduce a list of duties with "shall," make sure the ending phrases all fit well with "shall." Do not say, "The Treasurer shall: a) collect . . .; b) maintain . . .; and c) may appoint assistants." Make c), instead, something like: "appoint any assistants needed."

Duties of officers, directors, boards, and committees read best when they are phrased in terms of "shall," rather than "will." "Shall" has the connotation of "these are the rules you should follow," while "will" connotes more of an authoritarian tone of "You will do this or else."

When stating the duties of officers or committees, you can use one "shall" with a colon and set out the rest in separate paragraphs ending in semicolons without repeating the "shall." Just make certain the other phrases fit with the "shall." If that does not work, then use separate sentences listing the duties, but make them complete sentences. They will flow better that way.

Note: Strive for consistency of language.

▶ **Tip:** Use plenty of spacing between paragraphs, headings, and subheadings.

▶ **Tip:** Lists created as bulleted lists are easier to understand.

7

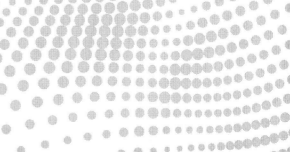

For some items, you can use "is" or "are." For instance, when you state the name of the society, "is" is fine. When you address officers' duties, "shall" is better because those duties must be carried out in the future on a continual basis. The name of the society, once chosen, will remain the same.

If you require notice to be given for some act, be sure also to specify by whom notice shall be given, by what method, and how many days' notice is required.

Note: It is a good idea to define "a member in good standing." Then, use the phrase throughout your bylaws with no misunderstanding.

Avoid referring to another specific article and section in a bylaws provision. It works fine when the bylaws are adopted, but you may later amend the referred-to section and forget to change the reference. You can avoid the problem by simply saying: "as provided elsewhere in these bylaws."

Organize your bylaws so the first time a concept or term appears, it is defined or stated in such a way that its meaning is clear. Later references can then merely state the term. Do not require your reader to wonder about the meaning for three pages until the term is finally defined.

Include your fiscal year in the bylaws (see Article IX under Dues and Finance), as well as your membership year. Any other pertinent calendar dates should also be included, so long as they do not commit you to dates for which you need flexibility. Items you can include are the time of the annual meeting and the date by which a budget must be adopted.

Weak: "A member *(singular)* shall receive their *(plural)* newsletter..."

Strong: "A member *(singular)* shall receive the *(singular)* newsletter."

Eliminate sexist language; happily, many societies have already done so. You need not use awkward terms such as his/her; there are many ways to avoid stating a gender. One of the easiest is simply to repeat the noun. Another is to reword the sentence so you do not need a pronoun. By the way, do not use a singular noun with "their"; it is grammatically incorrect. Reword the phrase instead.

8

Reconsider, however, using the term "chairman," a term that still appears frequently but has sexist overtones. "Chairperson" is a cumbersome substitute, but "chair" is a neutral term, and no one is likely to confuse the term when you also use it (if you do at all) to mean the person presiding at a meeting.

Note that "by a majority vote" already means a majority of those members entitled to vote who are present at a regularly or properly called meeting at which a quorum is present. Adding a qualifying phrase like "of the members present and voting" just makes the language redundant. The same rule applies to "by a two-thirds vote." And the term "a simple majority" is redundant; it is just a majority. Try to word bylaws in positive terms. Use "shall" rather than "shall not."

Avoid using the passive voice as much as possible. An active voice is more effective and makes for easier reading.

▶ **Tip:** Active voice is better than passive voice.

▦ **Passive:** "The quarterly shall be managed by the quarterly editor."

▦ **Active:** "The quarterly editor shall manage the quarterly publication."

9

Your goal in drafting bylaws is to make them sufficiently detailed so members will understand the basic structure and functions of your society, but you also need to make them as easy to read as possible. Ensure you capitalize the titles of officers and names of committees and refer to your society and board with a capital letter or you can leave all of them in lowercase. Do not capitalize "officers" or "directors" unless you capitalize the names of your other officers.

Eliminate redundancies. Put a provision in only one article and do not repeat it in another. Figure out which article it belongs best in and put it there; then adapt the other article so it does not need that provision or so that, at most, it has a reference to the other article.

⬤ **Note:** Do not put the provision citing the parliamentary authority in the meetings article. The parliamentary authority has its own article.

When writing, ensure that you write provisions that are positive, rather than negative. For example, provisions should direct what your society "shall do" rather than what the organization "shall not do."

- Check the individual sections of each article to make sure they belong. If they strike a jarring note, consider putting them in another article where they might fit better. Following the guidelines in this workbook can help you place provisions in the appropriate article.

Format

You can set up bylaws in a number of different ways. The important thing is to format them in a way that makes them easy to read. Set out each article separately and give each one a general name to make it easier for readers to locate specific articles. You can also set out sections within an article so each covers a separate item under that article. That helps when you are searching for a particular provision.

Use a word processing program to create and maintain your bylaws, ensuring that proper sections can be automatically numbered and placed in bold and italics for emphasis as needed.

In the interest of brevity and clarity, most examples of sections within an article in this workbook are single-spaced. Bylaws are easier to read, however, if you double-space individual sections.

Consider using indented paragraphs to list the duties of officers and committees. Some societies use hanging indents for each section so that "Section 1 [or A, or whatever you use]" starts at the margin, but the rest of the lines of the paragraph are indented. Experiment with different formats until you find one you like.

Numbering can be any style. You can use Arabic or Roman numerals or capital letters for the article headings. Just remember to alternate numbers with letters if you use some kind of outline style, starting with capital letters and then using lowercase letters.

Note: Every set of bylaws is different. Each organization is unique, reflecting that uniqueness in its bylaws. There is no one way that is "correct" in formulating bylaws. Following established guidelines using reputable references assures success.

11

Example:

Article: **III** *(Roman)*
  Section 1. *(Arabic)*
    a. *(lower case)*
    b.
    c.
    d.

The title of the bylaws is easy. Just do a variation of the following (preferably in larger size text to make it stand out):

BYLAWS OF THE (BLANK) GENEALOGICAL SOCIETY

If you say something about being a nonprofit, tax-exempt organization (although you really do not need to), the proper way to refer to the appropriate tax statute is: "the current version of Section 501(c)(3) of the Internal Revenue Code or the corresponding section of any future tax code." That statement allows for future statutory amendments that may change the section number; with this language, you would not then be required to amend your bylaws.

What not to include

As a general guideline, bylaws should not include any provisions that are considered to be standing rules. By definition, standing rules provide the details for administering a society. They enumerate items for which you might want an established structure, but also areas you recognize might change without affecting how your society really functions. Examples are the time of day, when, the place where your society has its general meetings, and the order in which meetings are conducted (which is generally covered by RONR) or the amount of dues set for this fiscal year. (You should not have to amend the bylaws to change the amount of your dues, but the bylaws should contain a provision on how and by whom dues get changed.)

Standing rules can be changed by the board or by the membership by means of a simple vote with no advance notice. Because bylaws are more difficult to amend, they should not include standing rules.

Your bylaws do not need to contain information already included in your Articles of Incorporation. These include items such as stating the location of the principal office of the society, provisions for changing the principal office, nontransferability of membership, members' right to inspect the corporation's books, nonliability of members and officers, naming of directors to satisfy your state's statutes on incorporation, and details about the corporate seal.

▶ **Tip:** Write positive bylaws.

■ **Weak:** "The society shall not offer programs espousing sloppy research methods."

■ **Strong:** "The society shall present programs that promote the highest standards of genealogical research."

13

Note: A constitution *and* bylaws is no longer necessary.

Having a separate constitution and bylaws is no longer necessary. Both documents are especially unnecessary if your society is incorporated. At one time, societies had both documents, with the constitution being harder to amend than the bylaws, but the Articles of Incorporation now fill that role. In most cases it is simpler to create and adopt a set of bylaws for your society rather than maintaining two separate documents.

Throughout this workbook are other comments about provisions that either should not be, or need not be, included in bylaws.

14

Completing your bylaws

Be sure to proofread the final document more than once. The best way to proofread is to have one person read every word and punctuation mark to another person. For that endeavor, use someone who is not a member of the bylaws committee. Even when you go over a draft a number of times, it is extremely easy to overlook an error, so find two detail-oriented people to proofread.

Look for inconsistencies between provisions. Eliminate such things as granting the president authority to appoint a committee in one section and granting the executive board the same authority in another. If you have referred to another article of the bylaws by a specific article number and section, make certain the reference actually appears in that article and section.

Besides proofreading for spelling and punctuation errors, you should read the bylaws carefully to be sure they make sense, say what they are supposed to say, and flow smoothly. A great way to check how your draft reads is to have people other than bylaws committee members read them. By the time you get to a final draft, your committee members inevitably will be heavily invested in its provisions and will no longer be very objective about them. Getting fresh people to read a draft can tell you whether there are inconsistencies, confusing sections, missing items, poor grammar, incorrect punctuation, and the like.

▶ **Tip:** The best proofreaders are individuals having had no involvement in the creation of the document.

15

Other society members can quickly tell you by reading the draft if they are able to understand how the society should operate; choose people who have not served as officers and do not already know how it should operate. Ideally, you should then find someone who enjoys writing and who understands the rules of grammar and punctuation to read the draft for language errors. With a careful attention to details you can easily create a nearly perfect set of bylaws to present to your membership.

16

Effective date of bylaws

Unless your bylaws provide otherwise, a revised set or any individual amendment becomes effective on the date the membership adopts it.

It is a good idea to date-track amendments to bylaws. If your society adopts a revised set, place the date of adoption at the end of the bylaws. When an individual section is revised subsequently, place "amended," together with the date, in parentheses at the end of the section.

Then you can tell at a glance when the current set was adopted and which sections have since been amended, and future revisers can easily follow their history. Examples: "(Adopted 1 January 1996)"; "(Amended 4 December 1995)."

▶ **Tip:** Create a footer on the bottom of each page of the entire bylaws document to record the effective date of the current bylaws. That way, you always know which version of the bylaws you are reading. This should eliminate referring to and using out-of-date bylaws.

ARTICLE I: NAME

Traditionally, the first article in a set of bylaws states the name of the society. It is not necessary to add the phrase "hereafter referred to as the Society," since it is perfectly clear that later use of the term "the Society" refers to your organization.

If your society is incorporated: The Articles of Incorporation (or the comparable name used in your state) will state the society's name, and it is redundant to repeat it in the bylaws, the title being sufficient to show the name.

Note, as a result, that the numbering of bylaws articles for an incorporated society will not correspond to those for an unincorporated society.

Additional items, such as, "a nonprofit corporation," "a nonprofit organization," and the address or location of the principal office of the society belong in the Articles of Incorporation, not in the bylaws.

The bylaws really are not the appropriate place for a history of your society, a listing of its charter members, a statement as to when and where it was incorporated, or a statement that it is a nonprofit organization within the meaning of Section 501(c)(3) of the Internal Revenue Code.

Example:

The name of this organization is the Blank Genealogical Society.

The name of this organization shall be St. Clair County Genealogical Society, hereinafter called the Society.

(St. Clair County Genealogical Society)

Note: State the name of your society exactly as written in the Articles of Incorporation. This becomes the official name of your society.

ARTICLE II: PURPOSE(S)

Can also be referred to as "Objects" or "Objectives." This section provides your members with a brief statement of your society's goals. Usually, a genealogy society has several goals; for easier reading, state them in paragraph format.

In most sections of the bylaws, rules are stated using "shall," particularly when speaking of officers' and committees' duties. For this section, however, "are" (assuming your society has more than one purpose) is better; when your society adopts the bylaws it means these are the society's purposes.

Draft your society's purposes from a broad perspective, encompassing the regional, national, and international flavor of genealogy today. State, for instance, that you aim to foster cooperation among all individuals interested in genealogy rather than stating that you will hold meetings with programs and instructions for your members.

If your society is incorporated: Strictly speaking, the purposes of your society are spelled out in your Articles of Incorporation and need not be repeated here. As a matter of reality, however, even if you supply your members with a copy of your articles of incorporation, almost no one will read them. Members might, however, read the bylaws, in which case, a statement of the purposes is worth repeating.

Note: Purposes should be broad in scope.

Weak: "The society shall publish a monthly newsletter."

Strong: "The society shall publish materials that feature state resources and records."

19

It can be especially useful to state your purposes in your bylaws even if your society is incorporated in the event the society was incorporated a number of years ago and its purposes now could be stated in more modern terms or if your Articles of Incorporation state only a broad, general purpose to comply with your state's laws on incorporation. Because the bylaws are your society's governing document, having a statement of purposes in them can be a useful reminder to officers and members of your society's goals.

Example:

The purposes of this organization are:
a) To assemble people who are interested in genealogy and in preserving family history,

b) To provide programs and publications for the instruction and education of interested persons, and

c) To help others gain genealogical information.

(South Bay Cities Genealogical Society)

Example:

The purpose of this Society is to promote genealogical research and education through:
1. Lectures, workshops, seminars, field trips, and the mutual exchange of genealogical material;

2. Creating and building interest in collecting and preserving historical records of this and related areas of [Your State];

3. Locating, cataloging, and preserving genealogical records and making them available to the public.

(East Cuyahoga County Genealogical Society)

Example:

The objectives of this Society are:
1. To promote an interest in genealogy;

2. To encourage and instruct members in genealogical research through careful documentation and the maintenance of quality genealogical standards;

3. To locate, preserve, and index public and private genealogical records [especially those of Your County] and to make those records available to members and to the general public;

4. To assist and support any genealogical library in [Your State] which is open to the public;

5. To publish genealogical and historical information in a regular newsletter and in any other publication as directed by the membership.

(Larimer County Genealogical Society Inc.)

Example:

The purposes of this Society are to encourage and further genealogical research through educational programs;

to exchange genealogical data among its members;

and to cooperate with regional, national, and individual societies with like purposes.

(Green Valley Genealogical Society)

Other individual ideas for purposes

Example:

To further genealogical research and promoting interest in family history.

To express the society's concern about records preservation and public access to records.

To establish and maintain a genealogical library through contributions, donations, exchanges, and purchases.

To improve the availability of and access to public records.

To locate, publish, and safeguard genealogical records, both public and private.

To bring together persons who are conducting genealogical research and to promote fellowship and cooperation among them.

To establish communication among those doing genealogical research.

To facilitate the study of genealogy and family history.

To encourage and provide support for the development of methods of researching, organizing, indexing, retrieving, preserving, and disseminating genealogical information and records.

For a surname organization

Example:

The purposes of the Society are the collection, preservation, and dissemination of genealogical and historical books, documents, artifacts, and information in any form concerning the [Blank] family in its various lines of descent.

(Blair Society for Genealogical Research)

21

For a statewide umbrella organization

Example:

The primary purpose of [Blank Umbrella Organization] is to improve communications among genealogical societies, libraries with genealogical collections, professionals, and the general public.

(Arizona Genealogical Advisory Board)

ARTICLE III: MEMBERSHIP

Qualifications for membership

The first section in this article should be a statement of the qualifications for membership in your society. It should also state the application and acceptance procedures, including which entity reviews and votes on applications.

If you desire to include qualifications for membership in your bylaws, ensure they remain relevant to your organization. Include items that are inclusive, such as "an interest in genealogy," or "a desire to preserve local records."

It is probably not a good idea to include a qualification such as "good character"; the bylaws would then have to state what that means and who determines it. It is probably better to give applicants the benefit of the doubt and to assume they are qualified if they are interested in genealogy. Besides, genealogy societies ought to be inclusive organizations rather than exclusive.

An optional section in this article is one on resignation and termination of membership for cause. Because many people join genealogy societies, in addition to the one where they live as they extend their family to a new geographical area and leave as they move on to other areas, it is generally understood that they can cease being members simply by not paying their dues at the start of a new membership year. Thus, a formal resignation requirement seems unnecessarily bureaucratic and more appropriate to less fluid organizations.

Note: Bylaws should contain provisions outlining disciplinary procedures. See "When disciplinary action is called for" on page 105. RONR has an entire chapter devoted to disciplinary actions.

It should be noted that many of the societies that submitted bylaws for this workbook have adopted provisions for this article that say who is eligible for membership, but have not also stated how an eligible person becomes a member. Both are strongly recommended.

Example:

Section 1. Any natural person interested in the purposes of the Society is eligible for membership and, upon acceptance by the Board of Directors and payment of dues, shall be admitted to membership.

(Lee County Genealogical Society Inc.)

Example:

Section 1. Membership is open to all persons and groups who are interested in genealogy and the Society's purposes. Any person who desires to become a member shall complete an application form and present it to the Registrar, with the required dues. All applications for membership must be approved by the Board of Directors.

(Arizona State Genealogical Society)

Example:

Section 1. Any applicant interested in furthering the objectives of this Society shall be accepted for membership upon submission of a completed application form and payment of dues.

(San Luis Obispo County Genealogical Society Inc.)

Example:

Section 1. A person shall be declared a member upon filing an application form and enclosing the payment of the annual dues for the first year.

(Polish Genealogical Society of America Inc.)

▶**Tip:** Offer special recognition to lifetime, patron, and honorary members. This encourages participation into these special categories. Confer honorary membership sparingly to preserve the honorific status of this category.

Classes of members

If your society has more than one class of members, the second section should list and define each class so the distinctions are easily understood.

The most common type of member, of course, is an individual (or active or voting) member.

24

Your society may also recognize family members, in which the second member of a household with an individual member pays reduced dues and the household receives only one copy of society publications. If you institute this class of membership, you will have to decide whether to limit the membership to husbands and wives or to extend it to other household members, such as siblings or a parent and an adult child.

Another type of membership is a lifetime membership, one for which a person pays a one-time fee (either a specified dollar amount or one stated as a certain number of times the annual individual dues) and becomes a member for life, never again paying annual dues but retaining full voting rights and privileges.

Occasionally, a society has a class of membership often referred to as sustaining or patron membership. The society may offer those memberships to institutions or businesses which make a donation to the society in a set amount but which do not thereby become active members. Alternatively, a sustaining member may be an individual who donates a set amount to the society each year over and above the regular annual dues.

Finally, your society may confer honorary membership (for which no dues are paid) on a long-time member who has been a faithful volunteer for many years or who has performed a great deed for the society. An honorary membership can also be conferred on a nonmember who has provided an invaluable service to the society.

Subject to the limitations of the bylaws, an honorary membership is perpetual. An honorary member has no voting privileges unless the bylaws so provide or unless the person is also a dues-paying regular member.

Your bylaws should state how and by whom an honorary membership is conferred.

Example:

Section 2. The categories of membership shall be as follows:

a. Individual Member. Any person who meets the requirements for membership and who has paid the annual dues.

b. Household Member. Additional individuals living at the same address as a member and who meet the requirements for membership may become members by paying one-half the annual dues. A household shall receive only one copy of Society publications.

c. Organization Member. Any organization which supports the purposes of the Society and which has paid the annual dues shall be a non-voting member.

d. Individual Lifetime Member. Any person who meets the requirements to become an individual member and pays one lump sum fee equal to twenty times the annual membership fee shall be a member for life. There are no household lifetime memberships.

e. Honorary Lifetime Member. Honorary lifetime membership is bestowed upon a person for exceptional service to the Society or to the theory and/or practice of genealogy. An Honorary Lifetime Membership shall be conferred after a two-thirds vote of the members of the Executive Board, followed by a two-thirds vote at a regular meeting of the Society. Honorary Lifetime Members are entitled to all the privileges of Individual Members but are exempt from paying dues.

(Fairfax Genealogical Society)

Example:

Section 2. There are six categories of membership:

a. Individual Membership: Upon the payment of annual dues and approval of the Membership Committee, individuals eighteen years or older may become members of the Society with all rights of membership, including the use of the Library of the Society and a subscription to the Society bulletin.

b. Joint Membership: Upon the payment of annual dues and approval of the Membership Committee, a husband and wife may become Joint Members with all rights of membership, including the use of the Library of the Society and one subscription to the Society bulletin.

c. *Sustaining Membership: A member in good standing may become a Sustaining Member and shall be excused from further paying annual dues while retaining all rights of membership by paying $500, being a member for ten continuous years or longer and paying $350, or by being a member for twenty-five continuous years or longer.*

d. *Life Membership: Upon written recommendation to and approval of the Board of Directors and a two-thirds vote at any regular meeting of the Society, a member who has contributed significantly to furthering the purposes of the Society may be awarded Life Membership and shall retain all rights of membership but be excused from further paying annual dues.*

e. *Honorary Membership: Upon recommendation of the Board of Directors and a two-thirds vote at any regular meeting of the Society, Honorary Membership may be conferred upon an individual who has made significant contributions to the Society. An Honorary Member has no right to vote or hold office unless the person also becomes a member of the Society.*

f. *Fellow: Upon recommendation of the Board of Directors and a two-thirds vote at any regular meeting of the Society, the designation Fellow may be conferred upon a member who has compiled and published genealogical or historical works or who is an eminent researcher of subjects within the purposes of the Society.*

(San Antonio Genealogical and Historical Society)

Example:

Section 2. The Society shall have two general classes of members: Yearly Members who shall pay dues once every year and Lifetime Members who shall pay dues only once upon becoming a member.

a. *Yearly Members are (1) Annual Members who pay their dues annually and (2) Contributing Members who pay their dues annually but who offer special financial support to the Society; both are entitled to vote and hold office.*

b. *Lifetime Members are (1) Life Members who pay dues only once upon becoming a member and (2) Patron Members who pay dues only once but who offer special financial support to the Society; both are entitled to vote and hold office.*

27

c. *The Executive Committee may confer an Honorary Membership upon an individual who has brought honor to the [Blank family] name. Honorary Members shall pay no dues and may not vote or hold office.*

(Blair Society for Genealogical Research)

Example:

(Note that the last category of membership is not defined.)

Section 2. There shall be four classes of membership:

Regular Member: A person who agrees to uphold the charter and bylaws of the society and who pays dues for the current year as fixed by the Board of Directors.

Associate Member: A person designated by a Regular Member as that person's Associate Member. Associate Members shall be entitled to all the rights and privileges of Regular Members except that they shall not receive publications and newsletters of the society.

Honorary Member: An honorary membership may be conferred upon any person whom the Board of Directors deems worthy of exceptional recognition. Honorary Members shall be excused from paying dues and shall have all rights and privileges of membership except the right to vote, hold office, or serve as a committee chair. The Board of Directors shall determine the duration of an Honorary Membership, which may be terminated by the member by paying annual dues.

Society, Family Association, and Institutional Members are eligible for nonvoting membership by paying annual dues.

(Durham-Orange Genealogical Society)

Example:

(Note that the three categories of the first class of membership are not defined.)

Section 2. There shall be four classes of membership:

a. *Annual members shall consist of those who pay annual dues within the following categories: Individual Membership, Individual and Spouse Membership, and Organizational Membership.*

b. *Distinguished Service Membership may be awarded to a member who has rendered continued outstanding service to the Society. Names must be submitted to and approved by the Board before presentation to the general membership for affirmation at a regular meeting. A majority vote will constitute acceptance of the candidate as a Distinguished Service Member. Those members shall be exempt from paying dues. The number of Distinguished Service Members shall not exceed ten percent of the total number of members.*

28

c. *Life Members shall consist of those individuals and spouses who elect to make a one-time payment of fifteen times the annual dues, which entitles them to membership paid in full for as long as they live.*

d. *Honorary Membership may be awarded to nonmembers who hold elected, appointed, salaried, or volunteer positions in other organizations, agencies, or groups and whose efforts in supporting the objectives of the Society merit distinction. Honorary Membership shall be conferred by vote of the Board and affirmation of the Society. Honorary Membership carries with it neither a dues requirement nor voting privileges and the designation shall cease to exist upon the individual's termination in the position held at the time the designation was awarded.*

e. *Individual, Individual and Spouse, Distinguished Service, and Life Members shall be entitled to vote, to hold office, and to participate in the business of the Society. An Organizational Member shall be entitled to designate a representative to act on its behalf. The representative shall be entitled to one vote, to hold office, and to participate in the business of the Society.*

(Eastern Washington Genealogical Society)

Example:

Section 1. Charter Membership:
   a. *All members who have joined the Society and who have paid dues prior to January 1, 1978.*

   b. *Charter members shall include individual or family memberships.*

(St. Clair County Genealogical Society)

Information on dues

Another section in this article should state any required fees (such as an initiation fee, something rarely required in genealogy societies and more normally applicable to fraternal organizations) and dues, the applicable time period for a dues payment (usually annually), the date by which members should be given notice of a delinquency, and the date after which a member will be dropped from membership for nonpayment of dues.

● **Note:** Bylaws should state when dues become delinquent and when members will be dropped from the membership roll.

▶ **Tip:** The dues fee structure should be in standing rules, where changes are more easily made.

29

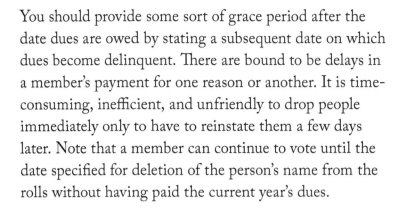

Note: A member in arrears still has a right to vote, unless otherwise stated in the bylaws.

You should provide some sort of grace period after the date dues are owed by stating a subsequent date on which dues become delinquent. There are bound to be delays in a member's payment for one reason or another. It is time-consuming, inefficient, and unfriendly to drop people immediately only to have to reinstate them a few days later. Note that a member can continue to vote until the date specified for deletion of the person's name from the rolls without having paid the current year's dues.

The specific amount of dues should not be stated in bylaws. If you state them, you will have to amend your bylaws every time you change your dues. Put the amount in the standing rules, and include a provision in your bylaws about how, when, and by whom dues can be changed.

(See also the examples under Article IX: Optional Articles, Dues and Finance)

Example:

Section 3. The dues shall be recommended by the Board of Directors and shall be approved by a majority vote at a regularly scheduled meeting. Annual dues shall be payable in advance on or before January 1. Dues become delinquent January 31, at which time the member's name shall be removed from the membership roll.

(Larimer County Genealogical Society Inc.)

Example:

Section 3. The amount of dues shall be established from time to time by the Board of Directors. Dues are payable in advance for the calendar year, and dues not paid by February 1 of each year are delinquent.

(Lee County Genealogical Society Inc.)

Example:

Section 3.
a. The Council shall recommend annually the dues of the Society and shall announce its recommendation no later than the third quarter of the year in an issue of the [Society bulletin] and/or the newsletter. Any increase in dues must be approved by a majority at the Annual Meeting.

b. Dues are payable annually on or before January 1 and are delinquent January 31. Members admitted after November 1 shall be credited with dues paid for the following year. The Registrar shall notify in writing by February 15 those members who are delinquent. Only paid members may hold office or be members of a committee.

(Iowa Genealogical Society)

Example:

Section 4.03 — Dues and Fiscal Year
B. Annual payment of dues shall be made no later than 31 January of each year.

C. If dues are not received by 15 February, the member shall be removed from the membership rules.
(Federation of Genealogical Societies)

Example:

Section 2. Resignation and Reinstatement
c. To be reinstated the member dropped for failure to pay dues must reapply as a new member.
(St. Clair County Genealogical Society)

ARTICLE IV: OFFICERS

Note: Four officers are the minimum number needed to effectively manage a society, no matter how small. A presiding officer and a secretary are required for every official meeting. Also, the president should not be the recorder.

Decisions

Your first decision, of course, is to determine how many officers your society will need to operate properly. If yours is a small society, it might function well with the traditional four elected officers: president, vice-president, secretary, and treasurer. Chances are, however, you will end up requiring a few more voices to be in charge. There are a number of options in that event.

One of the simplest ways to increase the number of voices governing a society is to provide for two or more elected directors-at-large. In addition to contributing more input to society decisions, directors can either be made chairs of or responsible for one or more standing committees. They can then serve as a pipeline between the committees and the governing board.

Other ways to increase the number of officers: split the office of secretary into two positions, a recording secretary who takes the meeting minutes and a corresponding secretary who handles society correspondence; add a registrar who is in charge of membership records; have two or three vice-presidents, each of whom is responsible for a particular major activity of the society; have the immediate past president continue to serve on the board for a term after the presidential term ends. You can provide, however, that the immediate past president be an ex officio member of the board; that way, the person can provide guidance and continuity but without a vote. In some cases, a governing board can become too large, resulting in a difficult decision making process for your organization.

If you are an existing society, you should examine the dynamics of your governing board to see whether it is the most efficient size for your society, both for getting things done and for avoiding problems of control by one person or a small group of persons.

If you are contemplating starting a society, ask existing societies about the advantages and disadvantages of the size of board they use.

Provisions

Your bylaws should state, at a minimum, the titles of your society's officers in descending order of rank. They also need to state how the officers are elected or appointed. Note that directors are usually considered to be officers; they need not be referred to separately when speaking of officers in general.

Example:

Traditional four officers:
Section 1. The officers of the Society shall be a President, a Vice-President, a Secretary, and a Treasurer. These officers shall perform the duties prescribed by these bylaws and by the parliamentary authority adopted by the Society.

(Polish Genealogical Society of America Inc.)

Example:

Additional officers:
Section 1. The elected officers of the Society shall be a President, First Vice-President, Second Vice-President, Third Vice-President, Corresponding Secretary, Recording Secretary, and Treasurer.

(Blair Society for Genealogical Research)

Example:

Section 1. The officers of the Society shall be a President, Vice-President, Recording Secretary, Correspondence Secretary, Treasurer, and Assistant Treasurer.

(Lee County Genealogical Society Inc.)

Example:

Section 1. The officers of the Society shall be the President, First Vice-President, Second Vice-President, Third Vice-President, Librarian, Recording Secretary, Corresponding Secretary, Treasurer, Immediate Past President and Member-at-Large, and three Trustees.

(Eastern Washington Genealogical Society)

Example:

Section 1. Elected officers of the Society shall be the President, Vice-President of Programs, Vice-President of Membership, Vice-President of Ways and Means, Recording Secretary, Corresponding Secretary, and Treasurer.

(San Luis Obispo County Genealogical Society Inc.)

33

Example:

Section 1. The officers of the Society shall be the President, Vice-President, Secretary/ Treasurer, Publicity Chair, a Michigan Genealogical Council representative, and an alternate representative. Any additional officers deemed necessary shall be elected by a majority vote at any regular business meeting.

(Eaton County Genealogical Society)

Example:

Section 1. The elected officers shall consist of the President, Vice-President, Secretary, Treasurer, Historian, Librarian, two Directors, and the immediate Past President.

(Genealogical Workshop of Mesa Inc.)

Qualifications of officers

You might also want to state qualifications for becoming an officer, usually the requirement that the person has been a member of the society for a period of time, a year, for instance. That provision can give your society some assurance that the person has some commitment to the society and to being an officer.

Example:

No person shall be eligible to hold office who has not been a member for at least six months prior to the nomination.

(Elkhart County Genealogical Society)

Example:

Only members in good standing may be elected to office or appointed to serve as committee chairs. The President shall have served at least one term in another position on the Board of Directors prior to being nominated for office.

(South Bay Cities Genealogical Society)

Example:

Elected officers shall have been members of the Society a minimum of two years, and the President shall have served previously on the Board of Directors.

(San Antonio Genealogical and Historical Society)

Example:

Only Active Members who are in good standing and who have belonged to the Society for at least one year shall be eligible to serve on the Board of Directors.

(Arizona State Genealogical Society)

Terms of office

Your bylaws should include a section on how long a term your officers serve, usually one or two years. To cover a possible emergency that prevents an election occurring on time, it is best to add the phrase "or until their successors are elected."

If you want your society to have term limits, such as providing that no officer may serve in the same office for more than two consecutive terms, include it here. Note that, under RONR, more than half a term is considered to be a full term. Provide as well for when the terms of office begin, whether it is at the end of the annual meeting or some later date.

You can also provide that no person can serve as an officer for more than a specified number of consecutive terms in any office; that provision helps alleviate the concern about one or more persons controlling the board (and, thus, the society) for many years. By expressing the limitation in terms of consecutive terms of office, you do not prevent anyone from serving as an officer, while at the same time you enable the opportunities for recruiting other qualified individuals who could bring a fresh perspective to the society.

If your society is concerned about continuity from one group of officers to another, you can provide for staggered terms. For instance, half your officers can be elected one year for a two-year term; the next year, the other half can be elected, also for a two-year term. That way, only half the board changes each year, and ongoing projects can sometimes be better managed. Note that if you choose this method, you need to consider which officers ought to be elected at the same time. If your president and vice-president are not elected at the same time, the vice-president can never succeed the president without creating a vacancy on the board of directors.

Another alternative is to elect your named officers for one-year terms and your directors for two-year terms.

You can also provide for officers to turn over records of the office to their successors within a specified time period after their terms expire.

▶ **Tip:** Consider staggered terms to provide continuity for changing officers.

Note: More than half a term filled (to fill a vacancy) is considered a full term when counting terms for term limits.

35

Example:

Section 2. Officers and directors shall be elected annually and shall hold office until their successors are duly elected and installed.

(Green Valley Genealogical Society)

Example:

Section 2. The officers shall be elected in November for a term of one year to begin in January; they shall serve until their successors are elected.

(East Cuyahoga County Genealogical Society)

Example:

Section 2. The officers shall be elected for a two-year term and shall serve until their successors are elected. Ideally, an officer should serve no more than two consecutive terms in any one office. All officers shall take office at the close of the Annual Meeting.

(San Luis Obispo County Genealogical Society Inc.)

Tip: Elect the president and vice-president in staggered years. This gives the new president an experienced vice-president to rely upon for advice.

36

Example:

Section 2. The term of office for the officers shall be one year, and they shall serve until their successors are elected. No member may be elected to serve more than three consecutive terms in the same office.

(Fairfax Genealogical Society)

Example:

Section 2. No elected officer shall serve more than three consecutive terms in the same office nor serve in more than one office concurrently, but may be reelected to the office after a lapse of two full years.

(Blair Society for Genealogical Research)

Different length terms for different offices

Example:

Section 2. The term of office for Board members shall be one year, and they shall serve until their successors are elected. No elected Board member may serve more than two consecutive terms in the same office, with the exception of the Librarian and the three Trustees. The term of office for Trustees shall be three years, with the term of one Trustee expiring each year.

(Eastern Washington Genealogical Society)

Note: The phrase "...or until a successor is elected..." means, if necessary, the officer may be removed before the term expires and replaced. The phrase "...and until a successor is elected..." means, if necessary, the officer must be removed by disciplinary means.

Example:

Section 2. The officers shall be elected for a one-year term, except for the Regional Representatives who shall be elected for a two-year term. No person may serve more than two consecutive terms in the same office, and no person may serve more than six consecutive terms on the Executive Council. The elected officers shall take office on January 1 following their election and shall serve until their successors are elected.

(Iowa Genealogical Society)

Staggered terms of office

Example:

Section 2. The President, Vice-President of Programs, Vice-President of Ways and Means, and the Recording Secretary shall be elected at the May meeting in even-numbered years. The Vice-President of Membership, Corresponding Secretary, and Treasurer shall be elected at the May meeting in odd-numbered years.

(San Luis Obispo County Genealogical Society Inc.)

Example:

Section 2. The President and the Recording Secretary shall be elected at the Annual Meeting in even-numbered years. The Vice-President, Corresponding Secretary, and Treasurer shall be elected at the Annual Meeting in odd-numbered years.

(Larimer County Genealogical Society Inc.)

Example:

Section 3. There shall be nine directors of whom three shall be elected each year to serve a term of three years. The term of office shall be on a calendar year basis. No director shall serve more than two consecutive terms in that position.

(International Society for British Genealogy and Family History)

Turning over records of the office

Example:

Section 7. The officers shall turn over all records and correspondence pertaining to the offices to their successors within fifteen days after their terms of office expire. An officer who resigns shall turn over all records for the office to the President within fifteen days of the resignation.

(Iowa Genealogical Society)

Example:

Section 4. Within thirty days after retiring from office, all officers shall deliver to their successors all monies, accounts, records, books, papers, and other property belonging to the Society.

(Arizona State Genealogical Society)

Example:

Section 7. All records of the outgoing Board members shall be transferred to incoming Board members no later than 1 January.

(Eastern Washington Genealogical Society)

37

Example:

> *Section 7. Upon retiring from office, all officers shall deliver to their successors all records and other property belonging to the Society.*
>
> (Eaton County Genealogical Society)

Example:

> *Section 8. New Executive Board members shall assume their positions at the beginning of the fiscal year following the meeting in which they are elected. Outgoing Board members shall turn over any files or records pertaining to their positions to their successors within thirty days of the election.*
>
> (Fairfax Genealogical Society)

Vacancies

Inevitably, your group of officers will change during the course of a term of office, because an officer moves away or becomes ill or passes away. Therefore, your bylaws should include a provision on how a vacancy is to be filled. There are several alternatives: the president can appoint someone with the approval of the board or the membership, the board can elect someone, or the membership can elect someone.

The method your society adopts depends on how much power your members have given your board and how often your board and your society meet. If your society meets only once a year or quarterly, it makes no sense to have the membership fill a vacancy. By the time the process is completed, the vacant term will have come to an end. Even if your membership meets monthly, it still might take two months to fill a vacancy, one to give notice of the vacancy and one to elect someone new. Deciding which method to use also requires an examination of how many activities your society has. If it has a large number, you may want to have the board fill a vacancy as quickly as possible so activities are not suspended for too long a period.

Note that, under RONR, a vacancy in the office of president is automatically filled by the vice-president. Even if you want the vice-president to fill the office, it might be best to state that in the bylaws for members who are unfamiliar with that rule. It is especially necessary if you have more than one vice-president; the provision then makes it clear which vice-president fills the vacancy.

Finally, you should provide that the person named to fill a vacancy serves until the end of the term remaining. The person is a substitute for the previously elected officer and serves the remainder of that officer's term.

Note: A statement that the vice-president shall assume the office of president in the event of a vacancy in that office can be placed either in the article on officers or in the article on the duties of officers.

Example:

Any vacancy occurring on the Board of Directors, with the exception of the office of President, may be filled for the remainder of the unexpired term by a majority vote of the remaining members of the Board of Directors.
(Arizona Genealogical Advisory Board)

Example:

Vacancies in any elective office shall be filled by approval of the Board until the next election, except the office of President, which shall be filled by the Vice-President. A new Vice-President shall then be chosen by the Board to serve the remainder of the unexpired term.
(Elkhart County Genealogical Society)

Example:

When a vacancy occurs on the Board of Directors, except for the office of President, that vacancy shall be filled by the membership at the first meeting of the membership following the vacancy. When a vacancy occurs in the office of President, that vacancy shall be filled by the Vice-President.
(Genealogical Workshop of Mesa Inc.)

Example:

With the approval of the Board of Directors, the President shall appoint a member to fill the unexpired term of any vacant office on the Board of Directors other than the office of President.
(Arizona State Genealogical Society)

Example:

The President shall appoint a person to serve in any office that becomes vacant. The person appointed shall serve until the end of the unexpired term. The appointment must be confirmed by a majority vote at the next Society business meeting.
(Fairfax Genealogical Society)

Example:

By election, the Board of Directors shall fill a vacancy arising in any office for the remainder of the term.

(Polish Genealogical Society of America Inc.)

Example:

In the event of a vacancy in the office of President, the Vice-President for Conferences shall assume the duties of the President. A vacancy in any other office shall be filled as the directors deem appropriate at the next meeting of the directors. It shall be the duty of the Executive Committee to act upon the resignation of any officer or director.

(Gentech Inc.)

Nominations and elections

RONR suggests placing provisions on the nomination and election of officers in the same article as the list of officers. That will work if you do not enumerate the duties of officers in your bylaws or if the enumeration you do include is quite brief. If you have a lengthy enumeration of officers' duties, consider placing the provisions on nominations and elections in a separate article.

● **Note:** The president should not influence the nominating committee, and by extension, the outcome of an election.

Nominating committee: Generally, your society's nominating committee should be elected by your membership or your board of directors or it may be appointed by the president with the approval of the board or the membership. That avoids any question of the president trying improperly to influence the election of officers.

▶ **Tip:** Established timelines keep the committee on track.

Your bylaws should include a provision on how and when the committee is selected. Note that a president is usually an ex officio member of all committees except the nominating committee. To avoid any question about that, spell out the exception in your bylaws.

● **Note:** The annual meeting is commonly the meeting for elections.

A nominating committee should contain an uneven number of members, usually either three or five. Normally, the first person selected for a committee becomes the chair. If you want to provide for another method of selecting the chair, you must spell it out in the bylaws. A current member of the board can sit on the committee unless the bylaws provide otherwise.

40

Provide as well for a timeline for the committee's functions. State when it should report to the membership. Be sure to have it selected at least a couple of months before it must report to give it time to find qualified officers. This is not a society function that should be performed in a hurry. Be careful not to rush through this process.

Decide, too, whether the committee should provide a list with one candidate for each office or can name more than one candidate for each office. That can be expressed by: "The Nominating Committee shall nominate a candidate for each office" or "The Nominating Committee shall nominate candidates for each office." Because it is probably not a good idea to require the committee to name multiple candidates for each office, you can instead say, "The Nominating Committee shall name one or more candidates for each office."

To avoid the committee's nominating a person who does not really want to be an officer, you can provide that the committee present as candidates only those who have agreed to serve.

Unless your bylaws provide otherwise, a member of the nominating committee can be named as a candidate for office.

Elections: If you have established one meeting a year as your annual meeting, you can provide in this article for holding the election of officers at your annual meeting.

If your society allows the elections to be held by mail, you need to include provisions on how that is accomplished. Be sure to state how much time before the election the ballots must be mailed to the members and when they need to be returned to the society.

Provide as well for counting the ballots, for instance, by the president appointing tellers to count them at the annual meeting and report the results.

Note: Bylaws must provide for electronic voting.

For information relating to electronic voting, be sure to examine "Voting and Electronic Voting" found in this workbook.

Example:

Section 1. The President shall appoint a nominating committee, with the approval of the Board of Directors, at the regular meeting in August. This committee shall nominate one or more candidates for each office.

Section 2. The slate of nominees shall be presented at the regular meeting in September. Following the committee report, nominations may be made from the floor.

Section 3. Ballots shall be mailed to all members in good standing at least twenty days prior to the October meeting and must be returned postmarked no later than seven days preceding the annual meeting in October.

Section 4. The nominating committee shall count the ballots at the October meeting. Officers shall be elected by a majority vote and shall take office immediately.

(South Bay Cities Genealogical Society)

Example:

(Note that Section 2 is ambiguous on the number of candidates for each office the committee can name.)

Section 1. At the September meeting of every even-numbered year, the Board of Directors shall elect a Nominating Committee of three, composed of one member of the Board and two non-Board members.

Section 2. The Nominating Committee shall prepare a list of candidates to fill all offices, having first obtained the consent of each such candidate. This list shall be recommended to the Society at the semiannual meeting in November when the election shall be held. Additional nominations from the floor shall be permitted.

Section 3. The Nominating Committee shall serve as the Election Committee. The chair shall serve as judge and the committee members as tellers. The Membership Chairperson shall distribute ballots to all members in good standing. A majority vote shall constitute election to office. If there are no nominations from the floor and if there are no objections by the members present, the Secretary shall be instructed to cast a unanimous ballot for the slate proposed.

(Polish Genealogical Society of America Inc.)

Example:

Section 1. The President, with the advice and consent of the Executive Board, shall appoint a Nominating Committee, consisting of three members, at least sixty days prior to the election meeting. No current member of the Board shall be eligible to serve on this committee.

42

Section 2. The Nominating Committee shall prepare a single slate of officers to be voted on by the membership at the election meeting.

Section 3. The Nominating Committee shall report to the membership at least fifteen days prior to the election meeting.

Section 4. Additional nominations may be made from the floor at the election meeting.

Section 5. No nominee shall be named, either by the Nominating Committee or from the floor, without having consented to serve as an officer.

Section 6. Officers shall be elected by a majority vote.
(Fairfax Genealogical Society)

Example:

Section 1. At the regular meeting each January, a Nominating Committee of five members shall be elected by majority vote by ballot. In years ending with an odd number, this committee shall nominate candidates for each elected office except those directors-at-large who shall be nominated in years ending with an even number. No member of the Nominating Committee shall serve consecutive terms. Notification of the election of the Nominating Committee shall be published prior to the January meeting.

Section 2. The Nominating Committee shall report at the February meeting, and the report shall be printed in the newsletter prior to the March meeting. Additional nominations may be made from the floor at the February and March meetings, and then the nominations shall be closed. Elections shall be held at the April meeting by ballot unless there is only one nominee for an office, in which case that election may be by voice vote.
(San Antonio Genealogical and Historical Society)

Example:

Section 1. A Nominating Committee composed of three members, the President excepted, at least one of whom shall have served on the Board, shall be appointed by the President, with the approval of the Board, no later than the September meeting. This committee shall submit a slate of nominees in writing at the October meeting. Nominations from the floor may be accepted at the November meeting. Any member of the Nominating Committee may also be a nominee. Each nominee must consent to be nominated.

43

Section 2. Elections of the Board members shall be in November and shall be conducted by the Elections Committee. Election shall be by secret ballot when there is more than one nominee for a position. If only one person is nominated for an office, the President may declare that person elected.

(Eastern Washington Genealogical Society)

Example:

Section 1. Nominating Committee. The Immediate Past President shall chair the Nominating Committee and shall propose committee membership to the Board for approval. The committee shall have a minimum of three and no more than seven members.

Section 2. Nominations. The Nominating Committee shall present nominations for officers and Board members to the Board for approval and shall publish them in the Society newsletter to notify the membership prior to the Annual Meeting. Nominations may be made from the floor at the Annual Meeting with the consent of the nominee.
Section 3. Elections. Officers and Board members shall be elected at the Annual Meeting by majority vote.

(Minnesota Genealogical Society Inc.)

Example:

(Note that Section 2 makes it unclear whether the committee names one candidate for each office or more than one.)

Section 1. At the March meeting, a Nominating Committee of five members shall be elected with two from the Board and three from the membership.

Section 2. The Nominating Committee shall report its slate of nominees at the regular meeting in April.

Section 3. The election of officers shall take place at the regular meeting in May at which time additional nominations may be made from the floor, provided the consent of the nominee has been secured.

Section 4. When more than one candidate has been nominated for an office, the election shall be by ballot and a plurality shall elect. When there is only one candidate for office, the election may be by voice vote and a majority shall elect.

(San Luis Obispo County Genealogical Society Inc.)

Example:

Section A. A nominating committee consisting of three members shall be appointed by the Executive Board in July of the election year (odd numbered year) to select a slate of officers and directors. The committee shall consist of at least one member from the current Executive Board, and at least one non-board member appointed from the general membership.

(Lake County Genealogical Society)

44

For a statewide umbrella organization

Example:

Section 1. The Nominating Committee, which shall consist of three members, one appointed by the Board of Directors and two elected at the Annual Membership Meeting, shall select and report the list of candidates to the Board of Directors in time for publication in the November newsletter.

Section 2. Nominations may be made from the floor at the Annual Membership Meeting, provided each nominee is present or has given written consent to serve if elected.

Section 3. Those members whose dues are paid in full may vote in elections. Member organizations shall have one designated representative with one vote on each issue. Member organizations shall advise the Membership Chair in writing of the name of the designated representative prior to any voting. Voting shall be by written ballot only. A majority vote elects.

(Arizona Genealogical Advisory Board)

Example:

Section 2. Officers
   a. The Directors shall determine officers.

   b. The officers shall be President, Vice-President, Chief Financial Officer, Treasurer, Recording Secretary and Corresponding Secretary.

   (California Genealogical Society)

▶ **Tip:** A nonboard member sitting on the nominating committee might consider persons not now in office. This could revitalize a society as new officers bring new ideas.

● **Note:** Some societies authorize the directors to select the society officers.

45

ARTICLE V: DUTIES OF OFFICERS

● Note: Officer subcategories (Corresponding Secretary, Recording Secretary, Vice-president of Administration, and Vice-president of Membership) require clear delineation of duties. Avoid misunderstandings due to assumptions.

▶ Tip: Clear definitions of officers' duties provides candidates a clear idea of what is expected of the office they seek.

If you have traditional officers whose duties are clearly understood and to whom you also assign a few duties throughout the bylaws, you can keep this article fairly simple. You may want to enumerate their duties however, so there are no questions about which officer is responsible for what duty. This is probably necessary if you have officers other than the traditional ones whose duties are not necessarily obvious from their titles.

If you list officers' duties, you can either do it in the article on officers in general or you can create a separate article in the bylaws for that purpose. In any event, if you list duties, be sure to add a provision at the end allowing for other duties to be added to avoid the (probably valid) claim that the listed duties are the only ones the officers can perform. Suggested wording: "and such other duties applicable to the office as prescribed by RONR. Note: That language will not apply to any officer other than the traditional four. If you have additional officers, you can use the following: "and such other duties as may be assigned by the Board of Directors or the Society."

If you decide to list officers' duties, make certain the list does not contain duties that are repeated elsewhere. If, for instance, you include in the president's duties the job of appointing standing committees, do not also provide in the article on committees that they are to be appointed by the president.

The easiest way to cover the issue is to include all the duties of officers in one article and to avoid restating one or more duties elsewhere. Bylaws are intended to be read as a whole, anyway, so it does not hurt if someone has to look at another section to see, for instance, how standing committees are appointed. Putting the duties all in one place also avoids the problem of ambiguity—when you list the duties in more than one place, you run the risk of creating questions about a duty because you probably will not say it in exactly the same way in both places.

When drafting a list of duties, however, keep the list as short as possible. Determine the three or four major responsibilities for each officer and put details about those responsibilities plus minor responsibilities in your policies and procedures manual. Your bylaws should merely cover the big picture. You might want to include a provision requiring your officers to present a written report to the membership at the annual meeting.

A note about the audit committee: A provision detailing how the audit committee is to be appointed and when it should report its results belongs in the article on committees, not in the article on officers' duties. When you list the treasurer's duties, you can require the treasurer to prepare the books for an audit at a certain time of year, but save the rest for elsewhere.

Note that only a few of the examples below include a phrase permitting the assignment of additional duties to the officers.

Example:

> *Section 1. The President shall be the principal executive officer, with responsibility for supervising the affairs of the society. The President shall preside at all meetings, shall appoint all committees with the approval of the Board, and shall be an ex officio member of all committees except the nominations committee.*

> *Section 2. The Vice-President shall assist the President and shall assume all duties of the President during the President's absence or inability to serve. The Vice-President shall plan and arrange programs and workshops for the society, subject to the approval of the Executive Board and in accordance with the interests of the membership.*

> *Section 3. The Corresponding Secretary shall handle all general correspondence of the society.*

> *Section 4. The Recording Secretary shall keep accurate records of the society's regular meetings and shall read the minutes of the preceding regular meeting during the business session of each regular meeting. The Secretary shall also keep records of Executive Board meetings and shall read the minutes of the preceding Board meeting during each Executive Board meeting.*

▶ **Tip:** Include a provision that authorizes the presiding officer, or similar authority, to assign duties "as needed" or "as necessary" to officers, directors, and committees.

47

Section 5. The Treasurer shall be the custodian of all revenues received by the society, shall deposit the funds in a bank approved by the society, shall pay all bills incurred by the society, shall keep accurate financial records, and shall maintain a record of society membership.

(Elkhart County Genealogical Society)

Example:

Section 1. The President shall be the principal executive officer of and the official spokesperson for the Society. The President shall preside at all meetings of the Society and the Council and, except as otherwise provided, shall appoint all committee chairpersons with the approval of the Council. The President shall be an ex officio, nonvoting member of all committees except the Nominating Committee.

Section 2. The Vice-President shall assist the President, shall assume the duties of the President in the absence of the President, and shall chair the Program Committee.

Section 3. The Secretary shall maintain a record of the proceedings of each meeting of the Society and of the Council and shall mail minutes of Council meetings within two weeks after a meeting to each member of the Council and the newsletter editor.

Section 4. The Treasurer shall have custody of the funds of the Society, shall have them deposited in a bank or banks approved by the Council, and shall make disbursements as directed by the Council. The Treasurer shall prepare and present a statement of financial condition to the Council at each meeting and shall give to the members a detailed statement showing receipts and disbursements for the year at the Annual Meeting. The records of the Treasurer shall be audited by March 1 each year.

Section 5. The Registrar shall be responsible for keeping a record of the membership of the Society, sending notices of delinquent dues, sending new member packets, and sending back issues of publications to new and renewed members. The Registrar shall chair the Membership Committee.

Section 6. The Regional Representatives shall act as liaisons between Chapters, members of the Society, and the Council and shall live in the region they represent.

(Iowa Genealogical Society)

Example:

Section 1. The President shall preside at all meetings of the general membership and the Board of Directors; appoint all chairs of standing committees, with the approval of the Board of Directors; with the Recording Secretary, sign all contracts and documents authorized by the Society; in the absence of the Treasurer, sign checks for authorized disbursements; serve as an ex officio member of all committees, except the Nominating Committee; and present a yearly report at the January meeting, which shall include highlights of reports of other Board members.

Section 2. The Vice-President shall assume the duties of the President in the absence of, or at the request of, the President; assume the duties of the President for the remaining term of office in the event of a vacancy in the office; and direct program planning to coordinate programs and speakers for general membership meetings, seminar speakers, field trips, and workshops.

Section 3. The Recording Secretary shall serve as the custodian of the Society's records, except those specifically assigned to others; keep a record of the proceedings of the Society; and with the President, sign all contracts and documents authorized by the Society.

Section 4. The Corresponding Secretary shall conduct the correspondence of the Society; notify the appropriate personnel of any special meeting; and pick up and distribute the Society's mail.

Section 5. The Treasurer shall **be the custodian of** *all funds of the Society;* **sign checks for authorized** *disbursements by the Society;* **present a statement** *of finances at each Board and* **general membership** *meeting; present a year-end* **financial report no later** *than the March Board and general meetings; present a proposed budget no later* **than the November Board** *meeting and a final budget to the membership at the subsequent Annual Meeting;* **and make all financial** *records available for audit six weeks before the March Board meeting.*

(Larimer County Genealogical Society Inc.)

Example:

Section 1. The President shall:

    a. preside at all meetings of the general membership and the Board;

    b. appoint all chairpersons of standing and special committees with the approval of the Board;

    c. sign all contracts and documents authorized by the Board;

49

d. appoint and chair the Budget Committee to prepare the annual budget for approval at the Board meeting held during the summer;

e. be the official representative of the Society, authorized to act on behalf of the Society; and

f. be an ex officio member of all committees except the Nominating Committee.

Section 2. The Vice-President of Programs shall:
a. assume the duties of the President in the absence of or at the request of the President;

b. assume the duties of the President for the remaining term of office in the event of a vacancy in that office;

c. arrange for programs for regular meetings;

d. provide information about future programs in a timely manner to the Publications Chairperson, Bulletin and Newsletter Editors, and Libraries; and

e. present an annual report to the President at the June Board meeting.

Section 3. The Vice President of Membership shall:
a. maintain the membership roster;

b. provide a renewal notice of membership dues prior to their expiration date;

c. provide current membership lists to Board members and annually to the membership;

d. provide mailing labels for the Society's bulk mailings; and

e. present an annual report to the President at the June Board meeting.

Section 4. The Vice President of Ways and Means shall:
a. submit plans for fund raising projects to the Board for authorization and coordinate the projects to completion; and

b. present an annual report to the President at the June Board meeting.

Section 5. The Recording Secretary shall:
a. record minutes of the proceedings of the Society;

b. keep and have available at all meetings the Articles of Incorporation, Bylaws, and Standing Rules; and

c. maintain a current inventory of all legal documents, records, and equipment belonging to the Society.

Section 6. The Corresponding Secretary shall:
a. conduct the correspondence of the Society;

b. maintain a monthly record of the Society's correspondence;

c. *pick up the Society's mail at the U. S. Post Office; and*

d. *notify the appropriate entities of any special meetings.*

Section 7. The Treasurer shall:

a. *maintain the records of all funds of the Society;*

b. *be responsible for depositing all moneys in the name of the Society in a federally insured depository designated by the Board;*

c. *pay designated line items in the annual budget when due and nondesignated line items as approved by the Board;*

d. *present a financial report and budget status report at each meeting of the Board and a summary of the reports at each general membership meeting;*

e. *serve on the Budget Committee;*

f. *prepare and present the financial records for audit after the end of the fiscal year and before the Annual Meeting; and*

g. *present an annual report to the President at the June Board meeting.*

(San Luis Obispo County Genealogical Society Inc.)

Example:

The powers and duties of the officers shall be as follows:

a. *The President shall be the executive officer of the Society, preside at all membership and Board of Directors meetings, appoint chairs of all standing committees, and be an ex officio member of all committees except the Nominating Committee. The President may appoint committee members, establish special committees, and call special meetings of the Board of Directors.*

b. *The Vice-President shall assist the President, perform the duties of the President when the President is absent, and succeed to the office of President in the event it becomes vacant.*

c. *The Recording Secretary shall keep the minutes of the Society and the Board of Directors and be custodian of all records not expressly assigned to others.*

d. *The Corresponding Secretary shall answer correspondence sent to the Society, maintain correspondence files, distribute all mail received by the Society, be responsible for the mailbox key, and direct the giving of notice of all Society meetings.*

51

e. *The Treasurer shall be the custodian of all Society funds, pay all bills authorized by the budget and the Board of Directors, present a proposed budget to the Board of Directors at its April meeting, prepare required financial reports, and prepare a financial statement at the end of each fiscal year.*

f. *The Registrar shall maintain membership records, collect dues, and present membership applications to the Board of Directors for approval.*

g. *The Directors-at-Large shall represent the will of the membership, respect the needs of the Society, and serve in such other capacities as the Board of Directors deems necessary.*

(Arizona State Genealogical Society)

Duties of other types of officers

Example:

The Librarian shall be responsible for acquisitions of the Society; processing and maintenance of materials of the Society; and the budgets of book and microfilm acquisitions, periodical acquisitions and binding, miscellaneous binding, and book drawing.

The Immediate Past President shall serve on the Bylaws Committee.

The Trustees shall act in an advisory capacity to the Board and the Society in all business matters.

(Eastern Washington Genealogical Society)

Example:

The Librarian shall oversee the operation of the library under the direction of the Board of Directors, be chair of the library committee, serve on the acquisitions committee, keep an accurate record of all acquisitions, report on activities at all membership and Board meetings, and submit a written report at the Annual Membership Meeting.

The Historian shall keep a written and pictorial record of the organization's activities and a file of all specially prepared materials distributed to the members.

Directors shall perform the duties assigned by the President and/or the Board of Directors.

(Genealogical Workshop of Mesa Inc.)

Example:

The Editor shall be responsible for editing and publishing the [Society bulletin] and shall select a staff to assist with publication of the bulletin and any other materials the Board of Directors may authorize.

(Genealogical Society of Riverside)

Example:

The Historian shall maintain the scrapbooks of the Society, maintain and preserve the records of the Society at the Library, and perform such other duties as may be assigned by the President, the Board of Directors, or the Society.

The Directors-at-Large shall be esteemed members of long standing who have contributed outstanding service to the Society and are dedicated to the purposes of the Society. They shall guide the Society in matters of general policy and perform such other duties as may be assigned by the President, the Board of Directors, or the Society.

(San Antonio Genealogical and Historical Society)

Submitting annual reports

Example:

Section 3. Members of the Board of Directors shall submit annual reports at the meeting in February. Reports shall include accomplishments and goals.

(Polish Genealogical Society Inc.)

Example:

Section 3. The President, Treasurer, Historian, and Librarian shall submit a full report of their activities for the past year at the Annual Membership Meeting.

(Genealogical Workshop of Mesa Inc.)

Example:

Section 2. The business meeting in May shall be the annual meeting at which reports of officers and of standing and special committees shall be heard.

(San Antonio Genealogical and Historical Society)

Example:

Section 2. The chair of each committee shall file with the President by February 1 an annual report of the committee's activities.

(Eaton County Genealogical Society)

Example:

Section 5. All officers shall present annual, written reports for acceptance by the Board of Directors at its April meeting. Accepted reports shall be presented to the membership at the Annual Meeting.

(Arizona State Genealogical Society)

Example:

Section 3. Duties
g. The Directors-at-Large shall be assigned duties by the President as needed.

(California Genealogical Society)

ARTICLE VI: MEETINGS

Note: The regular membership meeting is the heart of the society. Societies offer members the opportunity to learn from the programs, enhance their research skills by attending society-sponsored seminars, all while enjoying the fellowship of like-minded researchers.

Regular membership meetings

Your bylaws should provide for regularly scheduled meetings of your society. Be careful how you word this article. Under RONR if you set a day for meetings, such as "the second Tuesday of each month," and then add "unless otherwise ordered by the Society [or "by the Board"]," the Society or Board is then authorized to change only one meeting in unusual circumstances. Changes for more than one meeting require amendment of the bylaws.

Genealogy societies frequently do not meet each month. You can provide for that in your bylaws. A state society with many regional chapters may only meet quarterly or less often. A family name organization may only meet once a year or once every other year. That can also be stated in the bylaws.

The exact hour and precise location of your meetings should be included in your standing rules, rather than your bylaws to give your society flexibility in the time and place for meetings.

Provisions on meetings of your board of directors should appear in the article on the board.

Annual meetings

Generally, you will want to designate one meeting a year as the annual meeting. An annual meeting is generally required for corporations, but it is a good idea for unincorporated societies as well. The annual meeting is when officers are elected and annual reports are presented to the membership. It also serves as a reminder for societies to examine their bylaws, goals, activities, and accomplishments.

A separate section should be used to designate the time of the annual meeting, and a specific month should be selected so the meeting occurs once each twelve months. That is especially the case if your society is incorporated.

Special meetings

Occasionally, your society may need to hold a special meeting. Without a provision for special meetings in your bylaws, however, it cannot hold one. Therefore, your bylaws should state how and by whom a special meeting can be called. It is usually better to require that the members be given written notice of a special meeting. Be sure to include a minimum time period for the notice.

Under RONR, a society holding a special meeting can transact only the business for which the meeting was called, whether or not the bylaws so provide. Because many people do not know this, it is probably best to include a statement to that effect in the bylaws. Because of that rule, the notice of the special meeting should state the purpose of the meeting, and the bylaws should include that requirement.

Quorum

Your bylaws should include a section on how many members constitute a quorum for the transaction of business. If you do not adopt a rule, the required quorum is a majority of the members. For a large organization, many of whose **members do not attend** the meetings, which could pose **a problem. For that** reason, it is probably best to keep **the minimum** number rather small, something **considerably less** than a majority of your members. **On the other** hand, making it too small could inspire **a would-be** dictator. Avoid stating the **quorum as a percentage;** calculating whether the required **percentage is** present could take up valuable **time. A good rule of** thumb is to set the number at **the total members (not** guests) you can generally expect **to attend a regular** meeting of the society.

Even if your society is primarily run by the board of directors, you should provide for a quorum at membership meetings because certain matters require a vote of the membership, such as the election of officers and the amendment of bylaws.

Note: Quorum is taken at the beginning of the meeting. If someone leaves during the meeting and the quorum becomes deficit, but no one notices, the meeting may continue as usual.

55

It is advisable not to make the quorum the number of people present at a regularly scheduled meeting. That defeats the purpose of a quorum requirement, which, as RONR points out, is to protect the organization from totally unrepresentative action in the name of the group by an unduly small number of persons. If a quorum is not present, the only action that can legally be taken is to fix the time to adjourn the meeting, to actually adjourn the meeting, or to take measures to obtain a quorum.

Order of meetings

Do not include a list showing the order in which business is to be transacted at society meetings. That kind of list belongs in the procedures manual or you can make it a standing rule. The president is the only member who is usually concerned with the order of business so you may not need the list at all because RONR covers it well, but in any event, it does not belong in the bylaws. It is not really a governing rule for a society; it is simply a preferred procedure.

Regular meetings

Example:

Section 1. Meetings of the general membership shall be held on the second and fourth Fridays of each month beginning with the fourth Friday in September and ending with the second Friday in May. When a meeting date falls on a holiday, the Board of Directors shall set an alternative date.
(Genealogical Workshop of Mesa Inc.)

Example:

Section 1. Regular meetings of the society shall be held the fourth Thursday of the month, January through May, September, and October, and the second Thursday in December. The Executive Board, by a two-thirds vote, may, for extraordinary reasons, schedule a regular meeting at a different date.
(Dearborn Genealogical Society)

Example:

Section 1. The regular meetings of the society shall be held on the second Sunday of February, April, September, and November unless otherwise ordered by the Board of Directors.
(Polish Genealogical Society of America Inc.)

Example:

Section 1. Regular meetings shall be held monthly. The time and place of meetings shall be decided by the Executive Board.

(South Bay Cities Genealogical Society)

Example:

Section 1. A meeting of the general membership shall be held at least once each year. Such meetings shall occur in conjunction with an annual conference of the National Genealogical Society or the Federation of Genealogical Societies. The time and place of each meeting of the general membership shall be determined by the Board of Directors. Additionally special meetings of the Society may be called at any other time and place as shall be selected by the Board of Directors.

Section 2. Notice of all meetings of the general membership shall be sent to the all members by mail or electronic means at least 30 (thirty) days in advance of the meeting.

Section 3. For the purposes of conducting business, the members present shall constitute a quorum.

Section 4. Minutes of each meeting of the general membership shall be included in the next published issue of the Society's journal.

(International Society for British Genealogy and Family History)

● **Note:** Some societies meet only once a year. The bylaws need to make provisions for this unusual meeting circumstance: when are officers' reports due? audit report? elections?

For a family name organization

Example:

Section 1. A biennial general convention of the society shall be held in even years in the month of June. The place of the meeting shall be agreed upon by the members present at the previous meeting.

(Blair Society for Genealogical Research)

Annual meeting

Example:

Section 2. The regular meeting in June shall be known as the Annual Meeting.

(San Luis Obispo County Genealogical Society Inc.)

Example:

Section 2. The business meeting in May shall be the annual meeting at which reports of officers, standing, and special committees shall be heard.

(San Antonio Genealogical and Historical Society)

57

Example:

> *Section 2. The first meeting in December shall be the Annual Membership Meeting. Officers and Directors shall be elected at the Annual Membership Meeting.*
>
> (Genealogical Workshop of Mesa Inc.)

Example:

> *Section 3. Each member in good standing present at the Annual Meeting shall have one vote. No proxies will be accepted.*
>
> (California Genealogical Society)

For a statewide umbrella organization

Example:

> *Section 2. The Annual Membership Meeting shall be held in January to coincide with the January Board meeting.*
>
> (Arizona Genealogical Advisory Board)

For a state organization with chapters

Example:

> *Section 2. An Annual Meeting and Fall Conference shall be held in October or November or as determined by the Program Committee with the approval of the Council.*
>
> (Iowa Genealogical Society)

For a family name organization

Example:

> *Section 1. The annual meeting shall be held on the closest Saturday to Bunker Hill Day, June 17, or at a time and place decided upon at the preceding annual meeting.*
>
> (Bunker Family Association of America)

Special meetings

Example:

> *Section 3. Special meetings of the Society may be called by the President, the Board of Directors, or the written request of ten members. The call for a special meeting shall be given at least ten days in advance by written notice, which shall state the purpose of the meeting. No business other than that stated shall be conducted.*
>
> (Larimer County Genealogical Society Inc.)

Example:

> *Section 3. Special general meetings may be called with not less than five days' notice by the President and shall be called at the request of a majority of the Board of Directors or twenty-five members with not less than five days' notice.*
>
> (San Antonio Genealogical and Historical Society)

Example:

Section 3. Special meetings may be called by the President or by the written request of twenty members. The purpose of any special meetings shall be set forth in the notice of the meeting, which shall be mailed to all members in good standing at least twenty days prior to the meeting.

(South Bay Cities Genealogical Society)

Quorum

Example:

Section 4. At regular meetings, twelve members shall constitute a quorum.

(Durham-Orange Genealogical Society)

Example:

Section 4. The quorum for a meeting of the Society shall be twenty-five members.

(San Antonio Genealogical and Historical Society)

Example:

Section 4. For the purpose of conducting business, fifteen members shall constitute a quorum at any Society meeting.

(San Luis Obispo County Genealogical Society Inc.)

Example:

Section 4. A quorum at the regular meeting shall consist of fifty members.

(Eastern Washington Genealogical Society)

Example:

Section 4. Fifteen voting members of the Society shall constitute a quorum.

(Polish Genealogical Society of America Inc.)

Example:

Section 4. Ten percent of the paid-up members shall constitute a quorum at all general meetings of the society.

(Elkhart County Genealogical Society)

Example:

Section 3. Each member in good standing present at the Annual Meeting shall have one (1) vote.

No proxies shall be accepted.

(California Genealogical Society)

Note: RONR discourages proxy voting. It's a good idea to insert a provision that forbids proxy voting. This is one time when a "negative" provision is a good idea.

59

ARTICLE VII: BOARD OF DIRECTORS

Most societies also have a board of directors (also called an executive board or executive council) comprised of its elected officers and sometimes the immediate past president and/or chairs of certain standing committees. Try to keep the board a manageable size; if it is too large, it may be impossible for your society to accomplish anything.

You may want to include some appointed committee chairs on the board, but keep in mind that those people have not been selected by the membership at large. Create a board of directors that will effectively govern your society and its activities. You might pair committee chairs with officers so that the chairs report committee activity to their designated board member who then reports the activity to the board. Another option is to have an officer's duty include chairing a particular committee.

Once you decide your society will have a board, your next decision is the extent of its authority. You should determine whether the board will be authorized to act only between membership meetings (in which case, your bylaws should list the exact duties it can perform) or whether your board will basically run your society (in which case, your bylaws should provide it with a broad range of general powers). That decision will be based in part on the size and nature of your society. If your society seldom meets as a group, you will definitely need a board to run the society. The more often it meets, the less power may need to be given to the board.

Note: Some societies publish minutes of the board meetings in their newsletter. This keeps the membership informed of board activities and builds confidence in the board.

60

The nature of your society is also a consideration. If your members are primarily interested in a smooth-running organization with many activities, you may need a very active board to provide that. That is also true if your members would rather spend meeting time on a program than a business meeting. If your members do not want to vote on everything that comes along (which can take a lot of time from a program or other genealogically related activities), then give your board authority to govern fully, leaving for the membership matters such as annual elections, amending bylaws, and ratifying a dues increase.

Regardless of the power you give your board, remember that its actions cannot conflict with any action of the society unless your bylaws have given exclusive authority for that action to the board. Otherwise, the membership can vote to give the board specific instructions in a matter or to countermand some action by the board.

Provisions

Your bylaws should list the officers, directors, and committee chairs who make up your board; define its powers and duties; provide for meetings, both regular and special (remember that special meetings require notice; your bylaws should state a specified time period for the notice); state the number required for a quorum (generally a majority); and any special rules by which it operates.

Some societies also provide for removal of a board member if the person has a specified number of consecutive absences from board meetings. To avoid punishing someone who falls ill or who has a death or extended emergency in the family, you can make the absences required for removal unexcused ones. That permits a board member some flexibility during a difficult time period, yet still allows the board to remove a member who has lost interest in serving as an officer. You should already have a provision for filling vacancies in the article on officers; you need not repeat it here.

61

Note: Board quorum often states that at least two officers shall be included in the quorum count.

If your society is incorporated, you need not include a provision that the board shall constitute the board for purposes of your state's nonprofit corporation statutes. Your Articles of Incorporation will state what officers meet those requirements.

You also need not state that board members shall not be subject to liability for any actions they take on behalf of the society. Their immunity from liability is either inherent in the fact of incorporation (meaning your state's statutes on incorporating expressly provide that board members are immune) or is something that should appear in the Articles of Incorporation.

In addition, a society might want to indemnify the officers for any expenses they incur in responding to a law suit arising out of the society's activities. Even if a court should rule that an officer cannot be held liable for claims against the society, the officer would incur attorney's fees in obtaining that ruling. If the society agrees to indemnify its officers, the society would then pay the attorney's fees. An indemnification provision is something that also generally appears in the Articles of Incorporation. (Depending on your state's statutes, your society may be able to agree to indemnify its officers after suit is filed even if neither your Articles of Incorporation nor your bylaws contain such a provision.) Because the statutory provision on immunity and indemnification vary from state to state, this workbook contains no suggested provision on either. These are issues that, like the issue of choosing whether to incorporate in the first place, must be discussed with a lawyer familiar with the nonprofit incorporation statutes of your state.

Language giving the board the most power

Example:

The Board of Directors shall have full power and authority over the affairs of the Society except [list any type of business reserved to the membership].

(Robert's Rules of Order Newly Revised)

Language retaining full control in the membership, but giving the board power over details

Example:

> *The Board of Directors shall have general supervision of the affairs of the Society between its business meetings, fix the hour and place of meetings, make recommendations to the Society, and perform such other duties as are specified in these bylaws. The Board shall be subject to the orders of the Society, and none of its acts shall conflict with action taken by the Society.*
>
> (Robert's Rules of Order Newly Revised)

Example:

(Note that this example does not provide for special meetings of the board.)

> *Section 1. The Board of Directors shall consist of the elected officers.*
>
> *Section 2. The Board shall meet at least six times annually.*
>
> *Section 3. Three members of the Board shall constitute a quorum.*
>
> *Section 4. The Board shall:*
>
> > *a. transact the business of the Society between general membership meetings;*
> >
> > *b. direct committees; and*
> >
> > *c. approve general membership meeting programs.*
>
> *Section 5. Any member of the Board who fails to attend two consecutive meetings without an excuse acceptable to the Board shall be considered to have resigned.*
>
> (Larimer County Genealogical Society Inc.)

Example:

(Note that requiring two-thirds of the board members for a quorum may result in the board having to adjourn meetings because a quorum is not present. Note also that the provision on special board meetings does not provide for notice to be given to all board members.)

> *Section 1. Authority. Ultimate responsibility and authority shall reside in the Board, elected by and responsible to the membership. Day-to-day management shall be provided by the Executive Committee, whose actions are subject to approval by the Board.*
>
> *Section 2. Board membership. The Board of Directors shall consist of the officers, twelve directors elected by the Society, and the Immediate Past President.*
>
> *Section 3. Quorum. A quorum for Board meetings shall be two-thirds of the Board members.*

63

Section 4. Responsibilities. None of the Board's actions shall conflict with the purposes of the Society. The responsibilities of the Board shall be to:

a. establish policies of the Society;

b. direct the activities of the Society in a well-planned and practical manner for the benefit of the membership;

c. operate the Society as a nonprofit organization so that no part of its assets shall benefit any single individual;

d. assure that Society expenditures are allocated for educational purposes according to the requirements of the current provisions of the Internal Revenue Code for nonprofit organizations; and

e. establish, monitor, and adjust sound fiscal management policies.

Section 5. Meetings. The Board shall meet at least six times each year.

Section 6. Special Board Meetings. Special Board meetings may be called at any time by the President. Special Board meetings may also be called at the written request of six Board members to the President at least thirty days before the meeting.

(Minnesota Genealogical Society Inc.)

Example:

(Note that the provision on special meetings does not state a specified time period for giving notice of the meeting.)

Section 1. The members of the Executive Board shall be: President, Vice-President, Secretary, Treasurer, Immediate Past President, Education Chair, Membership Chair, Newsletter Editor, Publicity Chair, Records Chair, and Seminar Chair.

Section 2. The Executive Board shall meet at least quarterly at the call of the President. Any four members of the Board may, by written request, call a special meeting of the Board. A quorum for conducting business at any Board meeting shall be a majority of the Board members.

Section 3. The Executive Board shall administer and manage the business and affairs of the Society and shall be responsible for establishing policies and furthering Society purposes. The Board shall approve all committee and officer budgets and all individual expenditures not already approved as part of a committee or officer budget. The Board shall initiate an annual audit of the Society's financial records.

Section 4. Any action in which a majority of the Executive Board members shall concur in writing shall be binding and valid although not authorized or approved at a meeting of the Board.

Section 5. Any member of the Board who is absent from three consecutive Board meetings, without a reason determined by the President to be acceptable, shall be considered to have resigned from the Board.

(Fairfax Genealogical Society)

Example:

Section 1. The officers of the Society shall constitute the Board of Directors.

Section 2. The Board of Directors shall manage the affairs of the corporation, except as limited by law, the Articles of Incorporation, and these Bylaws.

Section 3. The Board of Directors shall meet once a month at a predetermined time and place.

Section 4. Special meetings of the Board may be called by the President or three members of the Board of Directors. All Board members shall be given at least five days' notice of special meetings.

Section 5. A majority of the members of the Board of Directors may transact business.

Section 6. Any member of the Board of Directors who is absent without excuse from three consecutive regular monthly Board meetings shall be deemed to have resigned from office, and the office shall be filled as provided elsewhere in these Bylaws.

(Arizona State Genealogical Society)

Additional provisions

Example:

Any action of the Board may be modified by the membership by a two-thirds vote.

(Eastern Washington Genealogical Society)

Example:

Any action required to be taken by law at a meeting of the Board of Directors or any action that may be taken at a meeting of the Board may be taken by a conference telephone call among a majority of the Board in which all persons participating can hear each other or without a meeting if a written consent stating the action taken is signed by all Board members and filed with the Secretary.

(Durham-Orange Genealogical Society)

65

For a family name organization

Example:

> *Proxy votes shall be allowed at Executive Board meetings to insure a quorum. A Board member who is unable to attend a meeting may assign the member's vote to another member of the Board, thus allowing the designated member to cast more than one vote.*
>
> (Blair Society for Genealogical Research)

Executive committee

Some societies may have an executive committee in addition to the board of directors. That is a group made up of a few of the top-ranking officers who may meet or confer between board meetings to transact pressing business. This type of group is necessary if your board does not meet monthly. If you decide to have an executive committee, provide for it in a separate article of the bylaws. That article should include the same types of provisions as you need for your board of directors.

Example:

> *Section 1. Membership. The Executive Committee shall consist of the Society officers, the Immediate Past President, and two members at large who shall be recommended by the President and approved by the Board. The President shall chair the committee.*
>
> *Section 2. Quorum. A majority of the Committee shall constitute a quorum.*
>
> *Section 3. Responsibilities. The Executive Committee shall carry out the policies of the Board between Board meetings and shall present programs, policies, and issues to the Board. Section 4. Authority. The Executive Committee shall exercise the authority granted it by the Board. The Committee shall report its actions to the Board at the next Board meeting, and the Board shall review those actions.*
>
> (Minnesota Genealogical Society Inc.)

Example:

Section 1. The President, Vice-Presidents, Recording Secretary, Treasurer, and Library Committee chair shall constitute the Executive Committee.

Section 2. The Executive Committee is authorized to act on behalf of the Society in matters of great urgency that occur between meetings of the Society or the Board of Directors.

Section 3. The Executive Committee shall report all actions taken at the next meeting of the Board of Directors.

Section 4. Five members of the Executive Committee shall constitute a quorum.

(San Antonio Genealogical and Historical Society)

ARTICLE VIII: COMMITTEES

Use your bylaws to establish standing committees you know your society requires. Those are permanent committees that perform various ongoing functions of your society. If you want those committees to have authority to act on matters related to their purposes without specific instructions from the society, you should list them by name in your bylaws. If you are assigning authority to the committee by naming it, you should also list the specific functions of the society that you are assigning to it.

Note, however, that if you list standing committees, those are the only ones your society can have without amending the bylaws unless you include a provision permitting creation of additional standing committees deemed necessary to carry on the society's work. Be sure to state what entity can create new committees—the president with approval of the board, the board of directors, or the membership.

You can also provide for special committees, ones that are created to fulfill a specific function and that cease to exist when they have completed their work and have reported to the appropriate entity. If you provide for special committees, just do it in a separate section of the article on committees. You do not need to put the provision in a separate article of the bylaws.

Under RONR, unless the bylaws provide otherwise, committees report to the membership, not to the board of directors. Unless the bylaws provide otherwise (and you will have to decide whether you want to provide otherwise), committee members serve terms that correspond with the terms of the society's officers or until their successors are selected.

Note: Standing committees are permanent in the organization. Special committees, also called ad hoc committees, are created to accomplish a specific purpose. A special committee is dissolved when the purpose is accomplished.

68

You will need to state how committees are selected. There are several options, including having the membership elect, having the board appoint them, having the president appoint them, and having the president appoint them with the approval of the board. You will need to select the method best suited to your society.

Electing each individual committee member can be a time-consuming process. In addition, the general membership may not have enough information about candidates to make a wise choice. They may also tire of having to elect not only officers but committee members as well. If you elect committees, the person elected first or the one with the highest number of votes becomes the chair, or the chair can be elected as a separate position.

Because many organizations find it difficult to obtain sufficient willing volunteers to serve on committees, it may be more efficient to have your president and/or your board of directors appoint them. The officers are more likely to know which members may be willing to serve and what their qualifications are. Note that the power to appoint a committee carries with it the power to appoint the chair and to fill any vacancy on the committee. If the entire committee is appointed, the first person named becomes the chair.

Some societies give the president the power to appoint committee chairs with the approval of the board and let the chairs choose the other committee members. Your bylaws may also provide that the duties of some officers automatically make them chairs or members of certain committees.

Your bylaws should name your standing committees, state their composition if necessary, provide for the manner in which they are selected (this provision may already appear in your article on officers' duties; if it does, do not repeat it here), and include a brief statement of their duties and authority.

69

To avoid being redundant, put the names and functions of the committees together. You do not need to name the committees and then list their duties in a separate section.

Example:

Section B. Each committee shall be guided by the Operations Handbook.

(Lake County Genealogical Society)

Example:

Section 1. Standing committees are permanent committees charged with performing necessary functions of the Society in a particular area. The standing committees of the Society and their duties are as follows:

  a. The Education Committee shall organize and present to members, the general public, or both, instructional classes and short orientation tours that pertain to the purposes of the Society. Its membership shall include the chairs of the Program Committee and the Seminar Committee.

  b. The Finance Committee shall function as both a short-term fund raising and long-range financial planning body to advise the Board of Directors, suggest and implement methods of raising money for the Society, and assist the Treasurer in preparing the annual budget.

  c. The Program Committee shall develop the annual program of events for the general membership meetings and present it to the Board of Directors for approval at or before the September Board meeting. Its membership shall include the chairs of the Education Committee and the Seminar Committee.

  d. The Membership Committee shall establish a program to encourage new members to join the Society and create an atmosphere of welcome for both members and guests at the general membership meetings.

  e. The Special Projects Committee shall present to the Board of Directors or the general membership worthwhile extraction projects of lasting value to the membership, other genealogists, historians, and the public and recommend to the Board of Directors publication of material that has been extracted.

  f. The Publicity Committee shall be responsible for all publicity and public relations for the Society. The Committee shall oversee the Historian who shall produce and maintain both a scrapbook about Society activities and a written and pictorial history of the Society.

● **Note:** It is recommended that you refer the details of the administration of the society (and its committees) to the standing rules, the policy and procedure manual, or any guidebook published by the society for its unique manner of conducting business.

70

g. *The Editorial Board, in accordance with the policies of the Board of Directors, shall determine and oversee the direction, tone, and content of all Society publications. The Board shall be composed of a chair who is not an editor of Society media, the editor(s) of the Society newsletter, the editor(s) of the Copper State Bulletin, and the chair of the Special Projects Committee.*

h. *The Seminar Committee shall conceive, plan, and conduct workshops and seminars for members and the public with the approval of the Board of Directors and in coordination with the Program Committee and the Education Committee. Its membership shall include the chairs of the Education Committee and the Program Committee.*

i. *The Vendors Committee shall establish policies and rules for and oversee the selling by vendors of items at general membership meetings and at seminars. The committee shall be composed of a chair and the chairs of the Program Committee, the Seminar Committee, and the Education Committee.*

j. *The Research Committee shall respond to research requests from members and the general public.*

k. *The Librarian shall receive and catalog exchange bulletins, flyers, and information pamphlets from other genealogical societies and organizations and shall make the materials available to the members.*

l. *The Parliamentarian shall advise the officers, board members, and general membership on proper parliamentary procedure and the requirements of the Articles of Incorporation, these Bylaws, and the policies and procedures of the Society and recommend additions or amendments to the Bylaws.*

m. *The Audit Committee shall consist of three persons, annually perform an audit both of the Treasurer's books and the Corresponding Secretary's log and an inventory of all Society property, and present a written report of its findings to the Board of Directors within sixty days after the close of the fiscal year. The committee shall also audit the Treasurer's books upon change of Treasurer and present its written report within sixty days after the change of Treasurer.*

71

n. *The Research Trip Committee shall organize and present to members, the general public, or both, research trips that pertain to the purposes of the Society.*

Section 2. The chairs of standing committees shall be responsible to the Board of Directors.

Section 3. All standing committees shall present written reports at the Annual Meeting.

Section 4. Special committees may be created to perform a specific function for a limited period of time.

Section 5. Chairs of special committees may be appointed by the President, a standing committee chair, the Board of Directors, or the general membership. The chairs shall be responsible to the person or entity that appointed them.

(Arizona State Genealogical Society)

Example:

Section 1. The Society shall have the following seven committees:

a. *The Finance Committee shall: prepare an annual budget each fiscal year and submit it to the Executive Committee for approval at least sixty days in advance of the fiscal year, oversee bonding of the Treasurer, arrange for an outside audit of the Society's financial records, suggest means of raising funds other than the membership dues, suggest ways to invest the funds of the Society, and perform such other services as may be prescribed by the Executive Committee.*

b. *The Membership Committee shall: be responsible for all advertisement of and publicity for the Society, act as liaison to other organizations that may have an affiliation with or interest in the Society, plan promotions to attract new members and retain present members, periodically survey the membership to determine if the Society is meeting its needs, and perform such other services as may be prescribed by the Executive Committee.*

c. *The Publications Committee shall: be responsible for selecting the format, contents, printing, and distribution of the Society's quarterly newsletter and its annual business report; solicit and assemble materials for these periodicals; suggest other publications for the Society to publish in order to meet its objectives; determine the format, contents, printing, and distribution of those publications; secure copyrights and insure that the copyright laws are observed; and perform such other services as may be prescribed by the Executive Committee.*

d. *The Program Committee shall: be responsible for suggesting sites for meetings, determining the time of meetings, assisting in securing accommodations and transportation for members, planning programs of interest to the membership, publicizing meetings, suggesting ways to create a closer bond of fellowship among members, purchasing the special awards given by the Society, and performing such other services as may be prescribed by the Executive Committee.*

e. *The Genealogy Committee shall: maintain a record of the lineage of each member of the Society, develop a system for matching lineages, distribute genealogical data and give research advice to the members, answer all queries from the members, and perform such other services as may be prescribed by the Executive Committee.*

f. *The Archives Committee shall: manage the archives of the Society, collect materials for inclusion in the archives, maintain a detailed inventory of all archival materials, insure that copyright laws are observed for such materials, search for records and documents not in the collection of the Society, undertake any special research projects on behalf of the Society, and perform such other services as may be prescribed by the Executive Committee.*

g. *The Nominating Committee shall: prepare a slate of candidates for the elected offices of the Society; submit this slate of candidates, accompanied by the written consent of each nominee, to the Executive Committee at least sixty days in advance of the election; seek out members who are qualified and willing to serve the Society either in an elected office or as a committee member; maintain a file of such members; and perform such other services as may be prescribed by the Executive Committee.*

Section 2. Each committee shall have no less than three and no more than seven members.

Section 3. The President shall appoint the chair of the Nominating Committee, and the Vice-Presidents shall appoint the chairs of the committees for which they are responsible.

Section 4. The chairs shall appoint the members of their committees, assign the duties of each member, submit a tentative budget to the Finance Committee at least 120 days in advance of the fiscal year, cooperate with other committees on projects of mutual concern, and insure that deadlines are met and reports are filed.

Section 5. The President shall be an ex officio member of every committee, except the Nominating Committee, and the Vice-Presidents shall be members of the committees for which they are responsible.

Section 6. No elected officer of the Society shall be a member of the Nominating Committee.

Section 7. All committees shall submit a quarterly summary of their activities and an annual report to the Executive Committee.

Section 8. The term of office of committee chairs shall expire when the elected officer who appointed them leaves office.

Section 9. The President shall create as many ad hoc committees as are deemed necessary to accomplish the goals of the Society.

(Blair Society for Genealogical Research)

Other types of committees

Example:

The Publicity Committee shall prepare and present to the news media notices and articles to keep the public informed of society activities.

(Dearborn Genealogical Society)

Example:

The Ways and Means Committee shall suggest and organize fund raising projects for the Society, to be approved by the Board of Directors.

The Publications Sales Committee shall sell all books, pamphlets, charts, and other materials offered by the Society; maintain the stock of sales materials; prepare an annual inventory of the stock; and keep accurate records of sales tax collected.

The Research Committee shall do local research for out-of-state members and for nonmembers. Any fees it earns shall accrue to the Society.

The Education Committee shall coordinate efforts to assist members in genealogical research, including, but not limited to, conducting classes and arranging educational trips and tours.

The Computer Genealogy Interest Committee shall hold semimonthly meetings for those interested in using computers to establish a genealogical data base. The committee shall aid in exchanging information, assist in the use of software, and help new users establish a genealogy data base.

(South Bay Cities Genealogical Society)

Example:

The Hospitality Committee shall assure the comfort of members and guests at meetings and be responsible for refreshments for meetings and special activities.

The Librarian shall: establish and maintain a systematic method of acquiring, cataloguing, and distributing books, pamphlets, magazines, reports, maps, and the like that make up the two genealogical libraries of the Society for the use of Society members and the public; maintain a current inventory of all library materials belonging to the Society; keep a record of all donations for books, films, and the like and an accounting of resale material and transmit the funds to the Treasurer for deposit; maintain records of the book funds and present accounting reports to the Treasurer; and present an annual report for each library to the President at the June Board meeting.

(San Luis Obispo County Genealogical Society Inc.)

Example:

Education Committee. The Education Committee shall be responsible for providing instruction in the use of proper genealogical research methodology and adherence to standards of accuracy and thoroughness in genealogical research to the members of the Society.

Program Committee. The Vice-President shall be the Program Chair. The Program Committee shall, in coordination with other affected committees, arrange for the program and the regular and special meetings of the Society.

Records Committee. The Records Committee shall: be responsible for preserving all records, manuscripts, typescripts, or published genealogical records received by the Society by gift or purchase; solicit gifts of, or purchase with the approval of the Executive Board, genealogical books, periodicals, and the like which may be of use to the members in their research; be responsible for arranging the deposit of Society genealogical records and books in appropriate locations; initiate and carry out activities to preserve and encourage the preservation of the genealogical resources of the Fairfax County area.

(Fairfax Genealogical Society)

Example:

The Editor/Editors of the Society newsletter shall: publish and mail the newsletter on a regular basis, collect and receive materials to be considered for publication in the newsletter, and publish in the newsletter any items specifically requested by the Board of Directors.

The Membership Committee shall: enroll all members and issue membership cards; maintain address files for current, past, and prospective members; and spearhead mailing campaigns.

The Publications Committee shall: receive materials for publication; coordinate the preparation of books, articles, and brochures for printing; and maintain an inventory of available Society publications.

(Larimer County Genealogical Society Inc.)

Example:

The Media Committee shall: be responsible for the sales table at meetings, conferences and workshops; process all media purchase requests; provide an inventory of the Society's media holdings; and, with Board approval, purchase all non-Society published media.

The Membership Committee shall: receive payments of dues, keep an account for each member, issue membership cards, and turn over monies received to the Treasurer in a timely manner.

The Research Committee shall maintain the Ancestor Index for research purposes.

The Publishing Committee shall prepare and publish a newsletter at least twice a year, a bulletin periodically, and other publications, subject to the approval of the Board of Directors. Periodical editors shall be members of the Publishing Committee.

(Polish Genealogical Society of America Inc.)

Example:

The Cemetery Committee shall maintain, preserve, publish, and sell records of Elkhart County cemeteries. The Chair shall be a member of the Publications Committee.

The Historical Records Committee shall be involved in compiling and preserving Elkhart County records and related materials of genealogical significance. The chair shall be called the society historian. The historian shall maintain scrapbooks of society activities and shall preserve society materials of historical significance.

The Publicity Committee shall be responsible for distributing news releases about society programs, workshops, and other activities to the news media and for sending notices of society functions to other historical and genealogical societies.

Two query chairs shall share responsibility for receiving and answering queries and for editing them for publication in the society quarterly.

(Elkhart County Genealogical Society)

Example:

The Book Selection Committee shall recommend to the Board of Directors the purchase of books, films, periodicals, software, and other research materials for the Society's Library, both from the Society's general fund and from funds contributed to the Society.

The Memorials Committee shall, in the event of the death of a member or of someone in the member's immediate family, encourage members to make donations to the Memorial Fund and shall ask the next-of-kin to select research materials to be placed in the Library that shall be purchased with the funds donated. At the direction of the Board of Directors, the committee may create special funds to receive donations of certain books and research materials.

The Property Committee shall: inventory all Society furniture, fixtures, and equipment and maintain a file of contracts for each item; coordinate the maintenance and repair of all Society furniture, fixtures, and equipment; and coordinate donations for and purchases of furniture, fixtures, and equipment.

(San Antonio Genealogical and Historical Society)

Example:

The Website Committee shall maintain the Society's website with items of interest to members and the public.

(Treasure Coast Genealogical Society Inc.)

ARTICLE IX: OPTIONAL ARTICLES

You can include other articles in your bylaws to cover circumstances applicable to your society. There is no limit on how many articles to include, keeping in mind, of course, that details on how your society should function belong in your policies and procedures manual and statements of policy on which the society needs to be flexible belong in your standing rules. It is best to keep your bylaws reasonably short so people are willing to read and follow them, but if you need bylaws-type rules beyond what RONR calls for, feel free to include them. Any additional articles should be placed before the articles on parliamentary authority and amendments to the bylaws, however. The amendments article should be last.

Dues and finance

One optional article that a number of societies include is one covering provisions about adjusting dues, handling the financial affairs of the society, adopting a budget, having the treasurer's books audited, and stating the fiscal year. There are no set rules on what to include in such an article. Choose from among the following examples provisions that appear to be useful to your society, remembering, as always, to make them specifically applicable to your society rather than just copying something down because someone else used it.

If you include rules about adopting a budget, be sure to state time periods for accomplishing the procedure, making certain it coincides properly with your fiscal year. One reason for stating the fiscal year in the bylaws is to remind officers about responsibilities that occur on an annual basis, e.g., adopting a budget and having the treasurer's books audited.

78

• **Note:** Some societies include a nonmember on the Audit Committee, even as the Auditor, to assure independence in evaluation of the society's financial documents and activities.

Do not allow too long a period for the books to be audited or it will be forgotten. Sixty to ninety days after the close of the fiscal year probably should be enough time.

Other titles for this article might be: Financial Management, Fiscal Matters and Audit, Fiscal Policy and Financial Management, Year and Dues.

Example:

Section 1. The operating expenses of the society shall be covered from collection of dues, donations, sales of publications, and such additional functions as the membership may authorize.

Section 2. The treasurer shall notify any member who has not paid dues by the December meeting of the expiration date one time in writing. Members still in arrears at the February meeting shall be removed from the membership roll. Suspended members will be reinstated after paying dues. Suspended members who pay dues after the end of the fiscal year shall be treated as new applicants for membership.

Section 3. Dues for the current fiscal year must accompany all applications for membership.

Section 4. The Executive Board shall designate the financial institution in which the funds of the society are to be deposited. The funds shall be deposited in the name of the society and shall be subject to withdrawals as authorized by resolution of the Executive Board.

Section 5. The fiscal year shall begin on July 1 and end on June 30 of the subsequent year.

(Dearborn Genealogical Society)

Example:

Section 1. Educational Disbursement Policy. Disbursements by the Society shall be made in such a manner that at the end of each fiscal year, at least fifty-one percent of all funds expended since the date of the Society's incorporation shall have been used in the State of Minnesota for educational purposes.

Section 2. Fiscal Year. The fiscal year shall be the calendar year.

Section 3. Annual Budget. The annual budget for the next fiscal year shall be approved by the Board no later than the last Board meeting of the current fiscal year.

Section 4. Dues. The Board shall recommend to the membership the amount for dues, which shall be set by the members by majority vote at any Society meeting. A notice stating the proposed dues structure shall be mailed to each member at least ten days before that meeting.

Section 5. Income and Expenditures. The Board shall establish orderly procedures for collection of all income. Authority for approval of all expenditures shall be defined by the Board.

Section 6. Auditing. The Board shall appoint a committee independent of the Board to audit the Society's fiscal records annually. This committee shall report its findings no later than the end of the first quarter of the next fiscal year.

(Minnesota Genealogical Society Inc.)

Example:

Section 1. The fiscal year of the Society shall be from June 1 to May 31.

Section 2. Accounts shall be in the Society's name only.

Section 3. An annual budget shall be prepared for approval at the Board meeting during the summer.

Section 4. The Treasurer, President, and Recording Secretary shall be authorized to sign checks, with only one signature required.

Section 5. The Librarian for each library may maintain a petty cash fund, in an amount to be determined by the Board, to pay small operational expenses.

Section 6. An Audit Committee of two or three members shall be appointed at the May Board meeting. The audit of the Society's financial records shall take place between June 1 and the Annual Meeting. The committee shall present its report to the general membership at the Annual Meeting.

Section 7. In the event of a vacancy in the office of Treasurer, a special audit shall be made before the new Treasurer assumes office.

(San Luis Obispo County Genealogical Society Inc.)

Example:

Section 1. The Society fiscal year shall be from 1 July to 30 June.

Section 2. The Executive Board shall approve an annual budget providing a specific amount for each committee or officer requiring Society funds.

Section 3. At such time as the President may direct, each committee chair shall submit a proposed budget for committee activities for the year, detailing briefly the amount desired and the purpose for which the money will be expended.

80

*Section 4. Committee chairs may authorize
expenditures up to the budget amount authorized and
for the purposes approved by the Executive Board.
Expenditures in excess of the budget allotment shall
be approved by the Executive Board, except that the
President may authorize additional expenditures not
exceeding $100, subject to ratification by the Executive
Board at its next meeting.*

*Section 5. The checking account established in the name
of the Society shall provide for signature on the checks by
either the President or the Treasurer.*

*Section 6. The Executive Board shall determine
annually an amount of funds to be placed in a
contingency, interest-bearing account. The officers shall
be listed as signatories, and two signatures shall be
required to make withdrawals. Use of these funds shall
require the approval of a majority of the Executive
Board.*

(Fairfax Genealogical Society)

Example:

*Section 1. The dues and annual contributions for each
type of membership shall be determined annually by
the Board of Directors before the start of each fiscal
year, shall become due and payable on or before the
next January 1, and shall become delinquent the next
February 1.*

*Section 2. Dues for new members shall be prorated on a
biannual basis, starting each July 1.*

*Section 3. The fiscal year shall be from May 1 through
April 30.*

*Section 4. The books and accounts of the Society
shall be kept in accordance with sound accounting
practices. At the end of each fiscal year, a copy of the
Audit Committee's reviewed financial report shall be
published by the Society.*

*Section 5. The President, the Vice President, and the
Treasurer shall be authorized as signatories on the
Society's accounts at financial institutions. The Board of
Directors may approve the creation of special accounts
and may authorize other members to be signatories on
those accounts.*

(Arizona State Genealogical Society)

Distribution of assets on dissolution

As a nonprofit organization under Section 501(c)(3)
of the Internal Revenue Code, your society is exempt
from paying income taxes so long as it is in existence
and continues to meet the requirements of the
statute. If the society should cease to exist, however,

any assets it had must be distributed to one or more other nonprofit organizations. You can add a provision covering that in your bylaws if there is a particular organization or organizations to whom your members would want the assets distributed. A court would take care of it in the event you make no provision (and might need to become involved anyway) so it really does not matter whether you include the provision.

If your society is incorporated, this provision belongs in the Articles of Incorporation, not in your bylaws.

A common error in drafting this provision is to simply copy some other organization's language verbatim. That may not work if the provision refers to a type of court that does not exist in your state. Make sure you adapt the provision to your circumstances.

A word about the Internal Revenue Code: The current version of the Internal Revenue Code was adopted in 1954; its provisions have, of course, been amended many times during the past many years. Because that may happen again and because the code could be completely revamped and a whole new version adopted, any reference to it in your bylaws should cover all contingencies. The appropriate reference is: "the current version of Section 501(c)(3) of the Internal Revenue Code or the corresponding section of any future tax code." Using that reference keeps you from having to amend your bylaws just because the tax code was amended.

Example:

In the event of dissolution of the Society, disposal of any remaining assets shall be determined by the Board in a manner most beneficial to genealogists and in accordance with the incorporation document. When a book donor has filed written instructions for this circumstance, those instructions shall be honored.

(San Luis Obispo County Genealogical Society Inc.)

Example:

In the event of the dissolution of the Society, any remaining assets shall be distributed to another organization of similar purpose or to a charitable organization, provided the organization is exempt under the current version of Section 501(c)(3) of the Internal Revenue Code or the corresponding section of any future tax code.

(Blair Society for Genealogical Research)

Example:

In the event of the dissolution of the Society, all salable assets shall be converted to cash. The monies of the Society shall be used to purchase genealogical materials for the genealogy division of a public library. Dissolution shall be conducted in accordance with the current version of Section 501(c)(3) of the Internal Revenue Code or the corresponding section of any future tax code.

(Larimer County Genealogical Society Inc.)

Example:

In the event of the dissolution of the Society, all funds and tangible assets shall be distributed at the direction of the Executive Committee to an Ohio organization or organizations exempt from taxation under the current version of Section 501(c)(3) of the Internal Revenue Code or the corresponding section of any future tax code.

(East Cuyahoga County Genealogical Society)

Example:

In the event of dissolution of the Society, the Board of Directors shall recommend to the Society at a regular meeting the disposition of the assets of the Society in accordance with the not-for-profit corporate statutes of the State of Texas, as amended, and the current version of Section 501(c)(3) of the Internal Revenue Code or the corresponding section of any future tax code. The disposition shall require the approval of the members by a two-thirds vote.

(San Antonio Genealogical and Historical Society)

Examples of miscellaneous provisions

Example:

Records and Documents. All records and documents sent to the Society, and all records and documents generated in the performance of duties on behalf of the Society, shall become the property of the Society and shall be given to the chair of the Archives Committee when they are no longer needed.

(Blair Society for Genealogical Research)

Example:

A document required to be executed on behalf of the Society shall be signed by two officers designated by the President as signatories.

(Eastern Washington Genealogical Society)

Example:

By joining the Society, members agree that any genealogical records they submit to the Society may be made available to any Society member or other researcher for research purposes. Members also agree that their names and genealogical data may be published in Society minutes or publications.

(Fairfax Genealogical Society)

Example:

Section 1. Each year, two months prior to the Annual Business Meeting the President shall appoint a Reviewer. The reviewer shall be a voting member of the Society and not a Member of the Board of Directors.

(California Genealogical Society)

Example:

Minutes of each meeting of the Board of Directors, the Executive Committee, and the general membership shall be made available to the membership within one month of the adjournment of the meeting.

Posting on the Society's website shall satisfy this requirement.

(International Society for British Genealogy and Family History)

Example:

Any Board member who has a financial, personal, or official interest in, or conflict (or the appearance of a conflict) with, any matter pending before the Board, of such nature that it prevents or may prevent that member from acting on the matter in an impartial manner, will vacate his or her seat and refrain from discussing and voting on the matter. The Board, at its sole discretion, may ask the member to remain for the discussion portion only.

(Computer-Assisted Genealogy Group of Northern Illinois)

ARTICLE X: PARLIAMENTARY AUTHORITY

Because a group should know the rules by which it functions, most genealogy societies adopt a parliamentary authority to govern in instances not covered by the bylaws. The accepted work for all types of organizations is *Robert's Rules of Order Newly Revised* (RONR). Although it can be difficult to read and sometimes deals with obscure matters probably foreign to genealogy societies, the book is an invaluable source for basic rules on how to conduct meetings, make motions, conduct elections, and the like.

Other alternative authorities include *The Standard Code of Parliamentary Procedure* (commonly referred to as Sturgis), though it often leaves room for more interpretation than RONR.

It is best to keep your bylaws flexible and refer to the current edition of the book **rather than to cite** a particular edition. The last **two phrases in the** example permit flexibility in **the event your society** chooses to do something in a **different way than** RONR.

Example:

(This is all you need for this article; *Robert's Rules of Order Newly Revised* says it best).

> *The rules contained in the current edition of Robert's Rules of Order Newly Revised, shall govern the Society in all cases to which they are applicable and in which they are not inconsistent with these bylaws and any special rules of order the Society may adopt.*
>
> (Robert's Rules of Order Newly Revised)

Note: This provision provides for the appointment of a parliamentarian and describes the consultative role.

Example:

The President shall name a Parliamentarian who will see that the rules contained in the current edition of Robert's Rules of Order Newly Revised shall govern the Society in all cases to which they are applicable and in which they are not inconsistent with these bylaws and any special rules of order the Society may adopt. The Parliamentarian advises the President and the Society at the meetings as needed and insures that the organization's rules are followed.

(Treasure Coast Genealogical Society Inc.)

ARTICLE XI: AMENDMENT OF BYLAWS

Although you will spend a great deal of time drafting an initial or revised set of bylaws, your society will inevitably need to amend them at some point. Therefore, the bylaws must provide for how those changes can be made.

Because bylaws are the basic governing document for your society, they should not be idly amended. Frequent tinkering with structure and procedure should be discouraged, and amendments should be carefully thought out and drafted.

At a minimum, your members need to be given written notice of any proposed changes, and the notice period should be sufficient for them to study the proposal and make a thoughtful decision about it. If your society meets monthly, you can require notice at the meeting prior to the one at which the vote will be taken.

If your society meets less frequently, the notice can be mailed to members a month or so before the meeting. Be sure to require notice at the previous meeting rather than a previous meeting; the latter has no time limitation. Requiring written notice assures that spur-of-the-moment decisions will not be made because the members only vote on the changes suggested in writing.

You can also provide for a procedure for bylaws changes by having a standing committee on bylaws that can periodically propose amendments. An alternative is for the board to appoint a committee to review the bylaws.

You can also provide that the board initially review or approve proposed amendments before they are submitted to the membership. Or you can permit amendment by any one of several alternative methods.

If you wish, you can limit voting on amendments to the annual meeting, but that can place a society in a difficult position if a change is seen to be needed shortly after the annual meeting. Waiting nearly a year for the chance to vote again could be detrimental to maintaining a well-run organization.

In keeping with the goal of making it difficult to amend bylaws, it is recommended that your society require a two-thirds vote to approve changes to bylaws. Note that you should require a "two-thirds vote" as opposed to a "two-thirds vote of the members." In a large organization, many of whose members do not attend meetings or actively participate, it could be next to impossible to obtain a two-thirds vote of the entire membership.

If your society has adopted *Robert's Rules of Order Newly Revised* as its parliamentary authority, the statement "two-thirds vote" automatically means two-thirds of the members qualified to vote who are present at a regularly scheduled meeting and who vote.

Note: Reviews of the bylaws about every five years is a good time frame. If needed, include new provisions to permit electronic voting and electronic meetings.

The requirements for amending any provision also apply to adopting a revised set of bylaws. However you word it, the amendment article should be the final one in your bylaws.

Example:

These bylaws can be amended at any regular meeting of the Society by a two-thirds vote, provided that the amendment has been submitted in writing at the previous regular meeting.

(Polish Genealogical Society of America Inc.)

Example:

Section 1. The Board shall determine when amendments to these bylaws are in order and shall instruct the Parliamentarian to form a committee to draw up the change(s).

Section 2. Written notice of the proposed amendment(s) shall be mailed to all members at least three weeks prior to the date of the vote.

Section 3. At the regular meeting following notification, a two-thirds vote shall adopt the amendment(s).
(San Luis Obispo County Genealogical Society Inc.)

Example:

Section 1. Amendments to the bylaws may be made as follows:

    a. Amendments to these bylaws may be originated by the Executive Board, the Bylaws Committee, or by petition signed by at least ten Society members. Amendments originated by the Bylaws Committee shall be approved by the Executive Board prior to their being submitted to the membership.

    b. Any amendment originating outside the Bylaws Committee shall be submitted to that committee in writing for review and for refinement into parliamentary language. The committee, in so doing, shall not change the essence of the proposal. The proposed amendment shall then be referred, with any recommendations, to the President for transmission to the Executive Board for its recommendation.

Section 2. Proposed amendments shall be reported to the entire Society membership in writing at least three weeks prior to the meeting at which they will be considered. Approval of amendments to the Bylaws requires a two-thirds vote at a regular Society meeting.

Section 3. Amendments shall become effective upon adoption unless otherwise specified in the amendment(s.)
(Fairfax Genealogical Society)

Example:

These bylaws may be amended at any regular meeting of the Society by a two-thirds vote, provided that the proposed amendments have been submitted in writing at the previous regular meeting and published in the newsletter prior to the meeting at which the amendments are to be adopted.
(San Antonio Genealogical and Historical Society)

Example:

These bylaws may be amended at any regular meeting of the Society by a two-thirds vote, provided that the proposed amendment has been:

    a. presented to the Board at any Board meeting and

    b. mailed to each Society member at least ten days before that regular Society meeting.

(Minnesota Genealogical Society Inc.)

Examples of restrictive procedures

Example:

Proposed amendments to these bylaws may be presented in writing to the Bylaws Committee before May 15 or must be presented to the Council no later than the July Council meeting. After approval by the Council, they shall be presented for a vote to the membership at the Annual Meeting. The bylaws shall be amended upon a two-thirds vote. Following the Annual Meeting, members shall be notified in a Society publication of the amendments approved.

(Iowa Genealogical Society)

Example:

These bylaws may be amended only at the Annual Meeting by a two-thirds standing vote, using the following procedures:

1. Proposals may be submitted in writing by any member to the Board of Directors at least four months prior to the Annual Meeting.

2. All proposed amendments, together with the recommendation of the Board of Directors, shall be presented to the membership at least two months prior to the Annual Meeting and printed in the newsletter just prior to the Annual Meeting.

(Larimer County Genealogical Society Inc.)

Dating your bylaws revision

This is where you show the date your bylaws were adopted.

Example:

Revised July 1, 1996

Example:

Bylaws adopted April 11, 1992.
Bylaws amendments adopted September 27, 1996.
Bylaws amendments adopted April 12, 2008.

(Colorado Council of Genealogical Societies)

Example:

REVISION HISTORY
Dec. 23, 1995
Mar. 13, 1999
Nov. 16, 2002
Sep. 17, 2005
Nov. 18, 2006
Jan. 20, 2007

(Computer-Assisted Genealogy Group of Northern Illinois)

To incorporate or not to incorporate

Introduction

Most individuals who become leaders in a genealogical society do so because they believe in the goals and programs of the organization and are willing to volunteer time and talent. Usually, their talents do not include knowledge about the Internal Revenue Service requirements for managing a nonprofit organization. However, learning even a few basic regulations will help both the volunteer and the organization avoid potential problems.

Decision-makers within an organization should first weigh the advantages and disadvantages of a nonprofit corporation.

Incorporation

Corporation: An association of individuals incorporated under the authority of state law.

Nonprofit Tax-Exempt Corporation: A corporation organized for nonprofit activity, with purposes that qualify it for exemption from paying federal corporate income taxes.

Advantages of a nonprofit corporation

• Lawsuits can be filed only against the assets of the organizations, not against the property of those who manage or belong to the organization.

• Incorporation protects the individual members from liability for acts performed in behalf of the corporation. If an accident occurs at a meeting or workshop, the individual members of the incorporated society will be exempt from litigations. This protection of the individual members is in itself worth the effort required to incorporate.

Note: This section is a reprint of the *Society Strategies Series* paper titled "Incorporation and IRS Regulations: Clarifying United States Non Profit and Tax Exempt Status" by Nancy J. Emmert. You may download a copy from http://www.fgs.org.

- An application can be filed with the Internal Revenue Service for tax-exempt status. Contributors to a nonprofit corporation with tax-exempt status may be able to deduct donations on their income tax returns (but this is true only if they itemize). This can be an important aspect to fund-raising.

- Most foundations and government agencies require that a society applying for funding or grants for establishment of a library or museum be a nonprofit, tax-exempt corporation. The organization should be incorporated if it owns a building to house a library, society office, or museum.

- People will more likely join a society that is a nonprofit, tax-xempt corporation because of the limited legal liability. They know that the society's Articles of Incorporation and bylaws conform to state requirements and that the society must maintain proper records, keep its minutes up-to-date, and abide by its bylaws.

- A society's status is increased in the community since other businesses and local government know they are dealing with an organization set up under law.

- A nonprofit society can apply for bulk-rate mailing privileges, allowing it to mail a minimum of 200 pieces of mail at a low rate. Mailing newsletters and quarterlies at bulk-rate will result in a savings over first-class mail rate.

Disadvantages of a nonprofit corporation

- A tax-exempt society may not work for or against a candidate seeking political office.

- A tax-exempt society is limited by federal regulations as to the amount which it can spend on lobbying to influence legislation or public opinion.

- According to law, standards for membership may not discriminate by race or sex. The society does have a right to require certain qualifications for membership, which may include geographical area.

- A society may be taxed on unrelated business income that exceeds $1000 and is not consistent with the stated tax-exempt purposes of the organization.

- No part of a nonprofit society's earnings can be distributed to its members. Proper expenses of officers and members can be reimbursed providing their activities further the purposes of the society.

- A society may be so small or its activities so limited that there is no need for formal incorporation.

- Dissolution is provided for by the laws of the state in which incorporated. A society should be certain that it is going to be in existence for many years if it incorporates, because the law requires that in the event the society dissolves, its assets must be given to another nonprofit organization.

Incorporation considerations

First, appoint a committee to investigate incorporation. They must consider such things as a proper name, the purposes, and necessary legal assistance. Incorporation is regulated by state law and differs in each. Write to the proper state authority, requesting all information, pamphlets, and sample Articles of Incorporation that are available.

Thoroughly investigate and acquire all necessary papers and information before consulting an attorney to draw up Articles of Incorporation under the "General Not for Profit Corporation Act."

Incorporation procedures

1. The name of the society must not be similar to another.

2. The purpose must be stated in the Articles of Incorporation. To apply for tax exemption later, the society must qualify as a tax–exempt organization.

3. Articles of Incorporation must be signed by the President or the Vice-President and the Secretary, one of whom is designated as the Registered Agent.

4. The Articles of Incorporation should be notarized.

5. The Articles of Incorporation are filed by mail or in person with the proper state office.

Requirements

1. The organization must have a specific nonprofit purpose as defined by Internal Revenue Service rules and fit into the categories it has established. A genealogical society will usually be classified as an educational organization under Section 501 (c) (3) of the IRS Code.

2. No one individual can benefit from the activities of the organization.

3. Lobbying cannot be a substantial part of the activities of the group.

4. The organization is not allowed to participate in political campaigns.

Application

A society which wants to apply for tax exempt status must use Form 1023 and pay a users fee. If the annual gross income of the organization is less than $10,000 over the last four years, the fee is $150. Otherwise, the fee is $500. IRS Publication 557, "Tax Exempt Status for Your Organization," details the requirements.

Organizations with less than $5000 of annual gross income are not required to file a Form 1023. However, if the organization has not filed the Form 1023 and has received a determination letter from the Internal Revenue Service, donations to the organization will not be deductible for income tax purposes.

Two books designed to explain and facilitate the process are *How to Form a Nonprofit Corporation* and *The Complete Guide to Nonprofit Corporations*.

State requirements

Each state has its own requirements for nonprofit and tax exempt status. Many will accept recognition from the Internal Revenue Service for this status. The publication, *How to Form a Nonprofit Corporation*, provides a state-by-state outline of these requirements.

Form 990

Societies with average annual gross revenues over $25,000 are required to file an informational Form 990 with the Internal Revenue Service. This is due by the 15th day of the 5th month after the close of the accounting year. An extension can be requested.

The IRS defines gross revenues as all of the money received in a year. A society which holds a workshop or conference which produces $25,000 of revenues, even with expenses of an equal amount, will probably be required to file the Form 990 because the amount of expenses are not considered when calculating gross revenue.

Unrelated income

Another type of income that can create potential problems is "unrelated income." This could occur if your group undertakes a fund raising project that is completely unrelated to your stated purposes.

Probably holding a genealogical conference, publishing and selling transcribed records, or designing and marketing forms would not cause a problem. If the fund-raising effort is done entirely by volunteers, again, it will probably not be treated as "unrelated income."

However, if your fund-raising activity—such as selling books which are not related to the purposes of your organization as are the genealogical ones—competes with for-profit business, this could create an "unrelated income" problem. The form 990-T would then be filed and income tax must be paid on the profits.

These basic principles of nonprofit and tax exempt status are management lessons all society leaders should know. Understanding and adhering to these regulations is your best insurance against potential problems with the Internal Revenue Service.

The Policy and Procedure Manual

Why is it important?

A policy and procedure manual contains a society's day-to-day business activities in a concise, consistent, textual format. It is a detailed expansion of the society's operating procedures or bylaws and is often called an operational handbook. All societies, whether large or small, should have a policy and procedure manual because it removes gray areas of assumed or ignored operation. It curtails hazardous management syndromes such as "Herd Mentality," "Reinventing the Wheel," "Let George do it," or "Nobody told me."

A policy and procedure manual is of great value to a society's board of directors, committee chairs, and other volunteers because it serves as a communications link, a timesaving aid, and a handy reference guide. It eliminates repetition, improves operational flow and is an immensely useful administrative tool.

It is helpful when training new officers and committees, and alleviates management frustration in the event of illness, death, or sudden resignation. It can also be a valuable asset to a nominating committee when assessing the qualifications of potential candidates by matching each to the clearly delineated job description. Additionally, a potential candidate can view the responsibilities of an offered position before deciding to accept the position. A procedure manual clears the way for more efficient operation of everyday activities and becomes a handy reference guide for society events, such as annual meetings or seminars.

While there is value in each officer and committee chair holding a separate section of the manual, it is more important that every officer and chair have a copy of the entire manual. A copy should be available in the society's office, the library, and at each meeting for society members to consult. A complete overview of how an organization functions increases a member's insight and awareness of the entire organization and promotes spirit and pride. This awareness improves overall efficiency and communication within an organization.

Development

How does a busy society develop such a tool? It does so by designing a manual that is not more, nor less than your own society needs. The table of contents to the procedure manual, for example, might carry only four sections, such as Officers, Committees, Special Committee(s), and Standard Operating Procedures (SOP). The basis for all segments of this suggested procedure manual, except the SOP, comes from the society bylaws.

The job of each officer and committee chair is treated individually in a procedure manual. Therefore, the first step in preparing the manual is to request each current officer and chair to set forth—in writing—a detailed job description. Involving the current and available past officers, board members, and committee chairs in a brainstorming session(s) offers the opportunity to tap into the collective knowledge of the society. The object is to provide the exact information another individual would need to suddenly take over a society position. Job descriptions also serve as reminders to current job holders of their duties.

Note: This section is a reprint of the *Society Strategies Series* paper titled "The Policy and Procedure Manual" by Martha L. Henderson, Betty R. Kaufman, and Paula Stuart-Warren, CG. You may download a copy from http://www.fgs.org.

97

First, list all past policy decisions that pertain to that job (include the date of the pertinent minutes for future reference). Next, list the exact bylaw quotation for that job. Finally, list in numerical order the principle responsibilities explicitly detailed in a job description or list specific duties and procedures. Include how the officer or chair reports to the board and at the annual meeting. This report should also define authority and clarify the working relationship with other elected or appointed position(s) to prevent infringement upon others or the overstepping of boundary lines. Include any standard forms used by this individual in this position though another officer/chair may also use part or all of the forms. Subcommittees of that officer/chair are developed on a separate page.

Keep in mind that the major goal in preparing a description of each society position is to outline everything about one specific job, such as policies, governing rules from the bylaws, job description, forms used, and subcommittee information.

Arrangement and format

A coordinator (usually the person in charge of society operations) analyzes each job description and cross-checks them for any duplication of effort or for ways to streamline operation. Development should be in accordance with the society bylaws and *Robert's Rules of Order Newly Revised.*

Create a separate page for each officer or chair should contain standardized headings. The overall arrangement of the officer and committee sections is the same order as listed in the bylaws. Each officer's job description is compiled in the "Officers" section. Committee descriptions appear in alphabetical order under the Committee section. Subcommittees should follow the appropriate committee description. The Committee section should conclude with an alphabetical listing and description of special committees. Forms that pertain to committee assignments should be placed within the appropriate description.

The Standard Operating Procedures section contains copies of the following documents:

- The Articles of Incorporation and any amendments
- IRS 501(c)(3) designation
- Authorization for a bulk permit; trade name registration; state sales tax exemption form or any other operational document
- Current bylaws
- ISBN and/or ISSN number
- Organizational charts
- Budget
- Board policies such as who has keys to the post office box, safety deposit box, etc.
- Bad weather notification policy
- Board and annual reports (number of copies and to whom)
- Publication schedules for newsletter and quarterly

Depending on its size, the SOP section of the manual could have its own brief table of contents. Another handy referral sheet for this section is an index to the forms found throughout the procedure manual.

Changes and updates

Board action is required to change policies. Changes in job descriptions, however, require less formal action because they are primarily functional duties. When a change is made in any phase of the operation, procedure manual updates are made by revising and distributing only the page or pages that pertain to the change. The revision must be dated to avoid later confusion. For example, the updated page(s) would state "Effective Date: 1 January 2002. Voids: 1 January 1999.

Calendar

A one-page calendar, compiled annually and inserted in the front of the procedure manual, is recommended. It shows all board and regular

Sample Policy and Procedure Manual Page

(NAME OF SOCIETY)

PROCEDURE MANUAL

Subject: Treasurer

Effective Date: 1 January 2005   Cancels: 1 January 2013

Distribution: All Officers and Committee Chairmen

TREASURER

POLICIES

- Budget/Finance—Treasurer monitors; Board controls
- Incidental bills exceeding $50 must be approved by Board; under $50 must be approved by President. (Minutes: 15 March 2001)
- May appoint assistant(s).
- Money raised by society must be used for educational purposes. (IRS Code 501(c)(3).)
- Notices for delinquent dues shall be given, and a report of such delinquencies due shall be provided to Membership Chairman and the Board. (Notice may be given via Newsletter.) [Use exact quote from bylaws.]

RESPONSIBILITIES

1. Custodian of all funds of the Society:

- Deposit all funds within two weeks of receipt.
- Pay all approved bills within one week of receipt.
- Keep accurate records of receipts and disbursements in society ledger book and checkbook and/or computer accounting program.
- Prepare Monthly Financial Report for Board and regular meetings.

2. Collect dues and issue membership cards; receipt provided upon request.

3. Maintain current membership list (IRS rule); deliver copy of monthly list of new and renewed membership to President, Membership Chairman, and Mailing List Chairman.

4. Serve as a member of Budget/Finance Committee.

5. Retain one (1) key to post office box.

6. Make all financial records available for audit six weeks prior to the Annual Meeting.

7. Present a financial report at the Annual Meeting covering the entire previous year.

meetings, legal holidays, special events and activities of the society. Also noted are deadlines, such as publication dates for the newsletter/quarterly, the dates when the nominating committee report and reports for when the annual meeting is due. A separate calendar for the treasurer would benefit others as well. It would show reports and payments of a less than monthly occurrence such as sales tax, bulk mailing fees and deposits, budget and finance meetings, and annual dues to other organizations.

Volunteers comprise the administrative body of a society. These individuals are busy people who respect and admire efficient organization. Handing a new volunteer an organized job description showing how the position fits into the operation of the society is very professional, as opposed to a folder or notebook of confusing, outdated, handwritten notes that take untold time to decipher and learn. To save money and time, subcommittee chairs are usually given only a photocopy of the page from the procedure manual that pertains to their particular job function. However, as an assurance that each volunteer knows his or her job and the jobs of others in the organization, it is recommended that the complete procedure manual be available at the society's office or library and at all meetings, and that each committee chair or board member bring the manual to all meetings, classes, etc.

A policy and procedure manual that is simple but thorough will keep a board of directors informed on society procedure and keep individuals informed on specific duties and deadlines. Each officer and director of even the smallest society should have his or her own copy.

Hierarchy of society documents

National, state, local laws

The highest authority for the society is the laws governing the state and region where the society is located. It would not be permissible to supersede the laws with bylaws that permit unlawful acts. While this makes perfect common sense, there might be instances were careless bylaw construction may actually violate state law.

Articles of Incorporation

The Articles of Incorporation are the next highest authority. These documents are the legal instrument which incorporates the society under the requirements of that particular state (or federal law in special cases). The articles contain the legal name of the society, and this is the name, exactly as recorded in the articles, that should be placed in Article I (Name) of the bylaws.

When a society becomes incorporated, the secretary of state's office registers the society and provides instructions for completing the required paperwork. Different states may have different requirements, but generally, the rules are quite similar. The requirements and documents for filing are easily accessible at the secretary of state's website.

Bylaws (Constitution)

The bylaws are the next authoritative document of the society. They define the primary characteristics of the organization rather than the parliamentary procedure it follows. They prescribe how the organization functions, and should include only the rules that the society considers so important that they cannot be easily changed.

It is rare nowadays to see the word "constitution" to denote a society document. It is an old term, now replaced by the term "bylaws." If a society wishes to retain the word "constitution" in association with the bylaws, there is no reason to remove it. It is perfectly acceptable, just rather outdated. The constitution formerly contained the first articles now in bylaws, and as such, was higher in priority to bylaws that contained the more administrative articles.

Special rules of order

Special rules of order are special parliamentary procedures adopted by the society and which supersede the parliamentary authority designated in the bylaws. These are rarely used in ordinary societies. An example of a special rule of order would be: "The society shall elect the officers by a two-thirds vote" (instead of the usual majority or plurality vote as stated in RONR).

Parliamentary authority

A parliamentary authority is the reference which organizations use to provide rules and guidance on meeting procedures that are not covered in the bylaws, standing rules, or policy and procedure manuals.

By far the most frequently used guide is *Robert's Rules of Order Newly Revised,* currently in its eleventh edition. Probably greater than 95 percent of societies cite this reference as their authority in their bylaws.

There are some other references out there, including: The *Standard Code of Parliamentary Procedure* (formerly the *Sturgis Standard Code of Parliamentary Procedure* by Alice Sturgis) was first published in 1950. Following the death of the author, the third (1988) and fourth (2001) editions were revised by a committee of the American Institute of Parliamentarians. This manual is commonly used in medical associations.

▶**Tip:** The website for the secretary of state offers useful advice on charitable organization setup. Most documents can be completed and fees paid online.

103

Demeter's *Manual of Parliamentary Law and Procedure*, by George Demeter, and commonly known as the Blue Book for its distinctive blue cover color, was revised in 1969. This manual is referred to by the American Institute of Parliamentarians and is the reference often cited by labor union associations.

Historic note: Thomas Jefferson's *Manual of Parliamentary Practice for the Use of the Senate of the United States*, written in 1801 while Jefferson was its presiding officer, was the first American book on parliamentary procedure.

Standing rules

Standing rules are rules related to the administration of the society, and not to parliamentary procedure. For example, the time at which a membership meeting will convene is a standing rule, but the motion that established the time for the membership meeting to convene is parliamentary procedure.

The policy and procedure manual is a standing rules document, it just has a different name. If your society has such a handbook, these are the standing rules of your society. You don't need to create another document called standing rules.

Standing rules should be the repository of those details which may change over time. These details require only a majority vote for adoption, unless the society adopts a special rule that states otherwise.

Custom

"That's the way we've always done it." This is a phrase we might hear when a member asks: Why do we do it this way?

A society may have a practice that works well, that's been going on for a long time, but has no written documentation. Customary practices that accomplish the task at hand and cause no disruption to society management has its place in the hierarchy of society rules.

When disciplinary action is called for

If it's been determined, usually by more than one person on the board, that a board member has offended the tenets of your society and that disciplinary actions are warranted, there is an outline of procedures, which you may pursue, and be assured that you are proceeding in the proper manner.

Many societies have in their bylaws their parliamentary authority as the current edition of *Robert's Rules of Order, Newly Revised*; disciplinary procedures are outlined in this book. Some societies have disciplinary procedures outlined within their bylaws....a good idea! Most bylaws, however, are rudimentary on this.

A society and its board have the right to make and enforce its own rules, and to require that its board members refrain from conduct injurious to the society. No one should be allowed to remain a board member of a society who violates the rules of good conduct and would possibly bring injury or bad name to the organization.

Offenses

What are some examples of bad conduct?

- An officer or board member who demeans, speaks derogatorily, or publicly criticizes the organization;

- a board member who discredits fellow board members;

- an officer who undermines board decisions and work;

- a board member who sullies the society's name and reputation.

Offenses can generally be separated into two categories: offenses occurring during meetings, and offenses occurring outside the meetings.

● **Note:** This section is a reprint of the *Society Strategies Series* paper titled "When Disciplinary Action is Called For," written by Roberta "Bobbi" King. You may download a copy from http://www.fgs.org.

Arguments and disagreements within the board must remain within the confines of the board room. Indeed, a good board should actively discuss the pros and cons of prospective board action and the merits of activities which affect the society.

But the public face of the ruling members of the society must be one of solid support for the society. When it appears that disciplinary measures need to be taken, tactful handling of the case is important, no matter how tempted you may be to talk about the offensive person and acts of misconduct.

Punishments that a society may impose include: suspension from the rights of membership (such as holding office), or expulsion from the organization.

Within a meeting

A board has the right to determine who may attend its meetings and has control of its meeting place. A board member of a society has the right—indeed the obligation—to attend meetings and participate in board discussions. A member, however, who has specifically been barred and forbidden to attend, cannot enter a board meeting. All members in a board meeting have the obligation to obey the orders of the presiding officer.

In a board meeting, a member who continues to speak when told to keep quiet, and who continues to disrupt the meeting, should be removed. A board member who speaks personally against other members of the society, by name and with clear disparagement, needs to be disciplined. A member who persists on speaking about irrelevant matters should be called to order and instructed to be seated. These troublesome members disturb the orderly conduct of business and generate an atmosphere of frustration and irritation on the board.

The presiding officer can instruct the secretary to record objectionable or disorderly words used by the member. The president might say: "Mr. Smith, I have warned you three times to refrain from negative comments about the Nominating Committee. Three times I have ordered you to be seated, but you continue to speak out of order."

If an unruly member quiets and sits down, and offers no further argument, the matter can rest.

Another member may, however, make a motion of "penalty"; he may make a motion that the member issue an immediate apology, that he leave the hall at this time, or that he be censured. A formal proceeding is presently "in effect" in the meeting setting. There are witnesses present, there are members who have seconded the disciplinary motion, and the present members make up the body which determines charges and penalties.

Strictly speaking, the presiding officer singularly does not have the power to remove a member from the room, but the board, as the governing assembly, does. If a member refuses to leave the meeting, the presiding officer, with judicious appraisal of the offense, can determine the action that best suits the situation. He can ask a committee of members to escort the offender to the door. These members have the legal right, parliamentary speaking, to use whatever force is necessary to remove the offender, but no more. This should always be the course of last resort; those individuals who applied unnecessary force could be liable for damages. After all, a person who would refuse to leave is likely the same type of person most likely to bring a lawsuit for damages, even with little justification.

The wise course would be to adjourn the meeting and pursue the matter in another way.

Outside the meeting

Society bylaws should contain an article specifying the offenses outside of the meetings for which penalties may be imposed; a statement such as: "any member found guilty of conduct tending to injure the good name of the organization, disturb its well-being, or hamper in its work" would provide a basis for disciplinary action. However, behavior of this nature is such a serious offense that it is definitely subject to disciplinary action, whether the bylaws mention it or not.

Since an organization has the right to describe its standards of membership, the board has a right to investigate matters which might be in violation of those standards. The information gained during the investigative process must not be made public, for confidentiality reasons. If it does become common knowledge within the membership of the society, it certainly must not go beyond the members.

After the investigative process is complete, the board does have the right to state that a member no longer has a position on the board. The society does not have the right to make public the specific charge which led to the expulsion, nor to reveal the details of the matter. To make any of the facts public, could constitute grounds for libel. A society's trial and investigation does not have the legality of a court of law; it can only establish the guilt of an accused and fitness for membership on the board.

A board member has the right to expect that allegations made against him must be brought on reasonable grounds. If a member is charged with a punishable offense, then he has the right to be informed of the charge, given time to prepare a defense, to appear and defend himself, and to be fairly and respectfully treated.

108

● **Note:** Board members and officers should always publicly support the society.

A member who is charged with an offense, in the face of numerous other members who are in agreement with the charges, may realize that submitting his resignation to the board may be a wiser course of action, rather than trying to fight the charge. It behooves the investigating committee to encourage the offending member, for the good of the society and all concerned, to offer his resignation quietly, before charges are preferred. Yes, the word is preferred. However, the board has no obligation to suggest, or even accept such a resignation at any stage of the case, even if it is submitted on the initiative of the offender.

Steps in the process of fair disciplinary action

A committee composed of board or society members, recognized for their attributes of fairness and evenhanded temperament, should conduct the confidential investigation. The inquiry should include an interview with the accused to determine if further action is warranted, including the advancement of charges. The investigative committee has no authority to require the accused, nor any other society member, to submit to an interview. The investigation should quietly pursue the gathering of relevant facts.

After investigation, the committee should prepare its report either exonerating the accused member or, if no other course of action seems possible, recommending the adoption of resolutions that would call the member to task. The resolution should state that a meeting has been set in which the accused member may show cause why he should not be assessed penalties. The resolution would specify the misconduct, and specify the date and place for a meeting to take place. Thirty days is generally an appropriate time to allow the member to prepare a defense.

The charges should state the offense: the act or misconduct that brings about the possibility of penalty, and the specific action which demonstrates the offense. A registered letter must be sent to the accused, and a copy retained by the society secretary. At the time of notification, the member's rights are suspended (except those as relate to the special meeting and his defense).

The presiding officer of the special meeting should refrain from a prosecutorial tone to the meeting. His role is to see that fairness prevails and that a just outcome is the consequence of the preceding investigation. If the accused member fails to appear at the designated meeting, the meeting takes place without him. This meeting is in executive session: there is an obligation of secrecy upon the participants.

The meeting is called to order by the chair, who directs the secretary to read the charges (the offenses and acts of misconduct). The chair asks the accused if he is "guilty" or "not guilty" of the charges. If the accused agrees to guilt, then the meeting proceeds to a brief description of the facts, and then immediately on to assessment of the penalty. If the member states a "not guilty" claim, then the chair directs the proceedings in this general order:

1. opening statements from both sides representing the matter;

2. statements from witnesses of both sides;

3. closing arguments.

When closing arguments are complete, the accused must leave the room, and deliberations ensue. If the member is found guilty, the chair introduces the question of penalty, which is decided at this time (in the form of recommendations to the society). After these decisions are reached, the member is called back into the room and informed of the result.

The committee's report should be signed by all members of the committee and submitted, in writing, to the society, in executive session. The report would include the results of the committee vote, along with a confidential summary of the basis for the committee's findings, and the penalty recommended for the society to impose. The accused should be given the opportunity to write his statements about his case. When the society is ready to vote upon the recommendations, the accused leaves the room. The society can vote to impose the recommended punishment, to decrease the penalty, or to decline to impose the penalty, but it cannot increase the penalty. If the committee's recommendation was to exonerate the accused member, the society cannot impose any penalty.

Most of the time, society boards will meet and conduct their business with little or no disruption. However, on occasion, disciplinary problems may arise. It's a challenging situation when it becomes necessary to enact disciplinary measures against a board member, but a society must assure that order will prevail so as to maintain a strong and effective organization.

111

Electronic meetings

The ordinary society meeting, whether it's a small one as in a board or committee meeting, or is a large one as in a membership meeting, is the setting by which members meet in deliberative assembly within the hearing and sight of one another to discuss matters of importance and make decisions affecting the direction and health of the society. This is an essential characteristic of meetings.

The past several years have brought dramatic changes to the way we communicate.

Email, Skype, smartphones, cell phones with conference calling capabilities; these electronic modes offer instant messaging and opportunities for meeting together without leaving home.

Societies have started to take advantage of electronic meeting capabilities. With the higher costs of travel (gas, parking fees, meals, producing paper copies of reports, etc.), meeting electronically can be a more cost-efficient way to achieve the same purposes.

Executive committee meetings

Executive committees, commonly comprised of the few society officers, need to discuss the state of the society and formulate their recommendations and vision. They need to reach consensus and come to agreements within the small meeting in order to present a unified front to the board and membership. If there are disagreements among the officers, better to work out the conflicts in private and arrive at agreement than air the discord in front of the board and membership, revealing fractures in leadership and creating an impression of incompetence and pettiness.

This is not to say that differences of opinion cannot be made known. An officer who holds an opposing point of view should present the case, but in a calm, studied manner that represents careful, thought-out reasons for the differing view.

Board meetings

Board meetings require the members to meet to discuss the state of the society, formulate long-range planning, and consider the ideas, suggestions, complaints, and needs of the society as a whole. The board is tasked with managing the society and keeping it a viable, vibrant, exciting place to be as they host programs and genealogical fellowship.

Board members should be listening to members of the society who have complaints (often valid ones), who want to have a voice in the direction of the society, and who have great suggestions for projects, resources, and proposals, but who do not wish to stand up and be noticed but rather, want the board member to carry forward the ideas.

Membership meetings

Membership meetings combine the social milieu of genealogists with the learning of the art. These get-togethers offer the members opportunities to learn more about the work with interesting programs and expert advice. There may be refreshments, snacks, or, as an annual event, a potluck in a more casual meeting where members can tell personal stories, share discoveries, and generally just enjoy a sense of togetherness and the warmth of congenial companionship.

Face-to-face meetings vs. electronic meetings

Face-to-face meetings put everyone physically in the same room.

Here, attendees have the opportunity to see facial expressions, hear the nuances of tone of voice and the sound of the speech, and detect a sense of the group. A president can discern the temper of the assemblage and guide the direction of the meeting accordingly. Electronic meetings do not allow a president to see if there is a lack of enthusiasm for the idea, sour faces throughout the room, or eyes downcast in a manner of dissent.

When an electronic remote meeting is convened, members of the meeting are alone, separated from the group, wearing headsets or otherwise connected to the meeting via audio (some with video capabilities). Skype is a common method for convening meetings, with audio over the computer, audio over the telephone, or audio and video capabilities together on the personal computer.

The electronic meeting attendees lose the advantages of the face-to-face meeting. The audio can be scratchy, hard to understand, and mask the identity of the speakers, a distinct disadvantage when you want to know who is speaking. The meeting might be delayed due to problems from inexperienced members who can't sign on quickly. Usually, only one person at a time can speak as the connection permits. Video conferencing offers a visual display of faces, but still, the whole physical presence is missing and the subtleties of body language are lacking.

The electronic meeting attendees, led by the presiding officer, still must abide by the fundamental principles of meeting management: distribution of an agenda, recording of the minutes, approval of the previous meeting minutes, motions made per parliamentary procedure, and debate on the topics. Reports must be delivered, now by electronic means. It's preferable to send out reports a few days ahead of time, which speeds up the meeting if all attendees are familiar with the reports and up to speed on current events.

Bylaws provisions

The bylaws need to contain sections providing for electronic meetings. General phrases, such as "electronic meetings" are understood by everyone and encompass audio, video, telephone, or the several variations of the meaning of the phrase.

The best place to write the sections permitting electronic meetings is in the Meetings Article. This should cover the board, committee, executive committee, and membership meetings.

Sample Agenda

(NAME OF SOCIETY)
BOARD MEETING
Smith Public Library
Smith, Tennessee
February 31, 2030

1.   Call to Order

2.   Approval of the Agenda

3.   Approval of the Minutes

4.   President's Welcome, Announcements

5.   Officers' Reports

6.   Directors' Reports

7.   Delegates' Reports

8.   Unfinished Business

9.   New Business

     a. NARA Fund raiser

     b. Bylaws Review Committee to be created

     c. Organize research trip to Salt Lake City

     d. 1960 census celebration

10. Upcoming Board meeting dates

     October 14, November 22, no meeting in December

11. Adjournment

Note: It's rare for an ordinary society to offer electronic meeting possibilities for the regular membership meetings due to the size of the group, but there are certainly exceptions.

Electronic meetings have eliminated cost and time commitment demands that accompany the responsibilities of serving as a society officer, director, volunteer, or anyone who needs to meet with a society group. The advantages cannot be ignored, and could make the difference between someone serving as a society volunteer or not accepting the position.

Each group must assess the pros and cons of face-to-face meetings versus electronic meetings, then amend the bylaws to define the new processes.

Voting and electronic voting

Fundamentals of voting

Every member has the right to vote.

No one can legally prevent a member from voting, including the right of the president to cast a vote. The old myth "the president cannot vote" is exactly that: a myth. The president may vote, at any time, period.

However, it's customary for the president not to vote in order to preserve an air of impartiality. The president may vote when the vote will affect the outcome: 1) when a vote will break a tie (an affirmative vote would adopt the motion, whereas no vote would fail the motion which, as a tie, lacks a majority to pass) or, 2) when the vote would change the result (an affirmative or negative would tie the vote, resulting in a failed motion because of a tie).

Likewise, a member sitting on a board or committee that is considering a course of action which would favorably affect the member (such as acquiring a contract that would financially benefit the member's company) can also vote, as a right of membership. But the member should refrain from voting, or recuse from the entire matter, in order to preserve the spirit of impartiality.

Conversely, a member cannot be compelled to vote. Abstention is simply a refusal to vote, and cannot be called into question.

Every member has the right to secrecy.

Every member has the right to secrecy of voting. Most of the time, ordinary voting takes place by voice vote, raised hands, or a rising vote where secrecy is absent. But when secrecy is important, a paper ballot has traditionally provided that accommodation (which any member can request, as a motion to vote by ballot). Ballot offers the member the right to not vote at all, to offer a write-in candidate, or to vote a preference.

One person is granted one vote.

Each member is allowed only one vote. This includes members who may hold more than one voting position, such as a vice-president who is also serving as the secretary pro tem. Technically, these are two voting positions, but only one person holds the spots, and only one vote is allowed.

Myth: The president cannot vote.

Fact: The president can vote, at any time, as a fundamental right of membership.

Electronic voting

When a society decides to go electronic, the bylaws need to be updated to reflect the new procedure. A general phrase, such as "...electronic methods..." can be used to encompass email, online voting, or website voting; any election that takes place that is not based on the traditional paper (and/or mailing) method and utilizing electronic communication methodology, would be considered electronic voting.

The procedures themselves should be put into the policy and procedure manual, or the standing rules. As the society figures out which methods work best for itself, the procedures can be easily modified and updated.

Board or committee vote

When a fairly small group, such as a board or committee, wishes to consider motions and vote electronically, the basic recommended procedure is this:

· Determine in advance the length of time for debate. Allow a few days for persons who do not check their communications daily to read the motion and have time to think about it. There needs to be a way for everyone to read all the comments and be able to contribute comments to the discussion.

- Determine in advance the person who shall be the timekeeper: someone who will monitor the time allowances for discussion, and for voting, who will close the communications at the proper time.

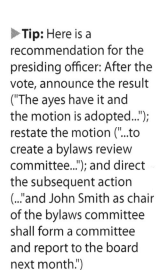

- Determine in advance the teller: the person who will receive the votes and report the results to the president.

- Determine a quorum in order to validate the vote.

- Treat each motion as one separate communication, with the subject heading "The motion to...." This makes it simpler for the readers to keep the motions separate (if there are more than one motion being considered); for the timekeeper to keep track of the time limits (several motions under consideration may have different time frames); and for the teller to keep track of the votes for each motion. This can make for a long thread of comments when 'Reply All' is used, but this is one way to deliberate and vote using electronic methods.

▶ **Tip:** Here is a recommendation for the presiding officer: After the vote, announce the result ("The ayes have it and the motion is adopted..."); restate the motion ("...to create a bylaws review committee..."); and direct the subsequent action (..."and John Smith as chair of the bylaws committee shall form a committee and report to the board next month.")

119

Membership voting

Generally, the only electronic voting performed by the entire society membership at one time would be the annual ballot for officers and/or the bylaw amendments. So a commercial enterprise may be the best solution for such a voting process in this case.

There are many commercial entities which offer voting services electronically. Many societies have found low-cost options that meet their needs.

Appoint a committee to research the available resources, keeping in mind the necessity for maintaining secrecy, permitting only one vote per person, and security for counting and reporting the votes.

Summary

The most important document for genealogical society members is the bylaws. This document informs members of a society about how the organization is supposed to function on a daily basis. The crafting of clear and effective bylaws is an important process that takes time and effort. Bylaws must be reviewed and often revised periodically. By using this workbook as a guide, societies can create a set of bylaws that will best serve their members and help them fulfill their mission.

Note: RONR discourages proxy voting. As your parliamentary authority, proxy voting would be prohibited in the society unless otherwise written into the bylaws.

Made in the USA
Lexington, KY
28 December 2012